What people say about the book, about Paul Shrimpling and about the work he does with accountants...

"Having known and worked with Paul for many years I am not in the slightest surprised at the quality of this most valuable book.

The book is a must-have addition to any accountant serious about assisting their clients to achieve their goals and build the life they desire and deserve."

Matt Donnelly, ad+ Chartered Accountants and Business Advisers, Glasgow, Scotland

*"**The Business Growth Accountant** is a treasure trove of advice on how to move your firm up the value curve – by giving your customers the services they need and want.*

In addition to Paul Shrimpling's sage advice – and here I will reveal my bias – be sure to pay particular attention to three more Pauls quoted in the book: the late Paul O'Byrne, RIP, and his partner, Paul Kennedy, who continues to run what I believe is the most innovative accounting firm in the world, O'Byrne & Kennedy; and, of course, Paul Dunn, the man who blazed the trail and helped thousands of firms fulfil the transformational journey that is energetically articulated throughout this book."

Ronald J. Baker, Radio-Show Host, The Soul of Enterprise: Business in the Knowledge Economy, and author of the best-selling Implementing Value Pricing: A Radical Business Model for Professional Firms, www.thesoulofenterprise.com, USA

"This is a truly brilliant Inspiring, Challenging and Supporting book from Paul that is a must read for every accountant in practice.

Even if you are not looking to become a "Growth Accountant" there are masses of ideas, tools, and tips you can implement in your practice to make your life easier and deliver a better experience to your clients.

Paul's story around "Canary-like" KPIs will stick with me forever and the section on "Blind, deaf and dumb pricing" has helped challenge the team on their communication skills. If you are in practice and want to make more of an impact in the lives of those around you this is a must-read book."

Simon Chaplin, Director of GreenStones, author and founder of SocksUpSimon, England

This book matters. And it matters because when you do what the book lays out for you, you will matter — as in seriously matter.

And that's stunningly important. Seth Godin says it like this, "The challenge is not to be successful, the challenge is to matter."

Just think about that for a moment. Perhaps even flip it around. When you do that you get that when you matter, success follows.

'Mattering' is essential. When you move from being dispensable to INdispensable, you matter.

Let me say it again: this book matters. when you do what it lays out for you, you will matter.

And like me, you'll thank Paul Shrimpling for making you matter, changing your life and the lives of those around you.

Paul Dunn, B1G1 Chairman and TEDx speaker

"Paul has packed this book with great detailed practical advice on a modern accounting business. It's jam-packed with insights on what you need to do to take your accounting business from where you are today, to where you want to be in the future. It's a must read, but more importantly, must action."

Steph Hinds, GrowthWise, Australia

"Paul has interviewed some remarkably smart practitioners, and blended their remarkably practical insights with his own, to produce a remarkably useful book"

Steve Pipe, Speaker, strategist and Amazon 5 star rated business author, England

"In one book, Paul has encapsulated, distilled down and enhanced a collection of disparate ideas from around the world. Ideas on the future of the accounting profession.

And in so doing he has pulled together the definitive how-to guide for the modern, evolving accounting practice.

One that works with technology, not one that is rendered irrelevant by it. One which is purpose driven. One which adds genuine value to its clients and the broader community. One which is distinctly profitable!"

Matt Paff, Value Adders Pty Ltd, Australia

"Brilliantly written, really easy to read, and bang on the money."

Paul Whitney, Director, Hallidays Chartered Accountants, Stockport, England

"Brilliant. I have sent this book out to the board of directors and all our team leaders.

The timing of this book is excellent as I have just started HIT (Hallidays Internal Training) which is a course on training client facing team members on how to be a great business advisor (not an accountant). This book reinforces and supports the learning in this programme. It is going to be essential reading for everyone attending.

This is incredibly valuable. I thought the chapter on questions was really interesting as I hadn't come across question frameworks before (maybe some of us don't need them!) and I think this will be a really useful chapter for the team members who choose to move from accountant to advisor.

I 100% endorse everything Paul talks about in this book – It felt strangely as if he'd been rummaging around in my mind and pulling loads of stuff out and putting it on paper!

But to summarise...

...essential reading for any accountant who truly cares about their clients and has a burning desire to do something to help clients more. The No 1 handbook for moving from accountant to (growth) advisor."

Nigel Bennett, Managing Director, Hallidays
Chartered Accountants, England

*"**The Business Growth Accountant** is a comprehensive, plain-speaking guide to profitability and advisory business growth. Many theorise about this – Paul tells you how!"*

Cameron John, Global Director of Accountant
Partners, Sage

4

"Having read Paul's book this has opened my eyes to the clear challenges that the profession faces. New technology and new competition mean firms need to seriously review what they do and how they do it.

The book clearly identifies these issues and provides guidance on how you can turn these into opportunities for the practice. This has inspired me to make the necessary changes in my practice to ensure its future and the exciting growth that can be achieved.

If you want to safeguard what you have and build on it, this book is a must read."

Daimien McConnell, ACA FCCA, William Hinton, England

"In this book Paul brilliantly articulates the key issues facing our industry and the most effective solutions to them from people who have done it already.

It took me years of reading, learning and conferences to work through them alone. If only I had had this manual earlier! He answers all the questions you might have but not the one that only you can answer for yourself: "Do I have the guts to try to make a difference to my clients' businesses?"

Luke Smith, FCA, Purpose, England

"If you're serious about growing and developing your accounting business, then Paul Shrimpling's book is essential reading. Don't just read it, take action. Do nothing at your own peril."

Greg Smargiassi , Managing Director, OurCFO, Australia

"It's time for accountants to do more for business owners than just do accounts and tax returns! Wherever you are in your career, this book will give you the confidence, insights and knowledge to do just that.

Easy to ready, it builds on your existing skillset. And, if you implement the ideas in the book, not only will it will position you as the go-to accountant, it will help you to make an incredible impact on your clients' businesses and the lives of so many, ultimately creating a better World."

Aynsley Damery, Director, Tayabali Tomlin, co-founder of TaxGo, England

"Paul's timely book – very readable and well presented – is another wake up call to the accountancy profession.

Change fast or become irrelevant. Your call. Simple as.

And Paul shows you how you can make significant change quickly so you will thrive. His guidance and advice has always been first class."

Seamus Parfrey, Parfrey Murphy Chartered Accountants, Ireland

"This is the book that the Accountancy Profession needs to wake itself up to what clients want.

It's all in the book - how you start and deliver Business Growth Consultancy to your clients. It's simply invaluable for those accountants that want to BE the change.

Well done Paul and this book needs to be read by every team member."

Rob Walsh, Managing Director, Clear Vision Accountancy Group, Wiltshire, England

"In his book Paul does not set out to be popular. He challenges you to be so much more than just another beige accountant. And let me tell you, the world doesn't need any more of them!

In your hands is the book that every dull, boring accountant should read so they get a sense of what the wise ones are doing. Then why wouldn't you leave mediocre and run-of-the-mill accounting behind you and take the actions and insights suggested by all the contributors to Paul's book?

If I were an accountant I'd buy every available copy of this book so that the competition can't get hold of a copy.

Paul, and the firms he's interviewed for the book, re-invigorate my belief that the accountancy profession can deliver on its potential to change the way that businesses perform."

Robert Craven, Managing Director, The Directors Centre, England

"I've just read Paul's book through and found it to be very engaging and, in places, challenging (in a good way).

I think the footnotes with links to online material really add to the value and I really liked the section on "Numbers To Grow By". Lots of material there that I will use.

I thought the Rugby story was a particularly excellent example of how changing the scoring (measuring) can change behaviour."

Clive Wilson, Director, Landmark Chartered Accountants, Watford, England

"Paul has an enviable reputation as a thought leader in the accounting world, and this book just goes to show why that is the case. He makes a compelling case for all accountants, large and small, demonstrating why they need to be looking at being advisors, not bean counters or tax return filers. What's more, he gives some simple nuggets of advice that are priceless."

Carl Reader, Director, D&T Chartered Accountants and Business Advisors, author and serial entreprenneur, The Startup Coach, England

"Having worked with Paul for a number of years and read many of the books, which are referred to here, it's great to see how Paul has pulled so much of this stuff together in one place. What is crystal clear and connected with me, is the importance of changing your mindset and being that advisor first, and an accountant second. We have already taken steps to reflect this and are changing our branding."

Alan Cowperthwaite, Director, Harvey Smith – Business Growth Accountants, England

"Having worked with Paul from afar, I can see that the dedication to his work is truly making a difference and inspiring the accountant's he works with. Which in turn is having an amazing impact on the client's that those accounting firms are working with.

Do yourself a favour, pick up this book and learn how you can create meaningful impacts in your accounting business which allow you to grow profitably. "

Trent McLaren, Practice Ignition, Australia

"I've just read the first 60 pages and thoroughly enjoying the book, I definitely agree with all the points you've made so far.

In January this year we launched our re-brand. We re-branded because any business that doesn't change with the times will be left behind and so rather than wait for change to happen we're working ahead of the curve. In a team session my opening slide said – Accounting isn't about the numbers, it's about people".

Having read your section on why perceived value stems from feelings, I'll tweak this slightly to 'people's feelings'. I'm looking forward to reading the rest of the book Paul. Thanks for the insight."

Elinor Perry-Hall, Managing Director, Pentlands Accountants And Advisors, Leamington Spa, England

"In my opinion this book is essential reading for any owner of an accountancy practice in these times where the pace of change is the fastest it has ever been. I have read a few books on the current issues facing the accountancy profession by different authors. The way this book has been put together, pooling a vast range of resources, ideas and research, provides a very good framework for re-modelling a traditional accountancy practice into a relevant advisory service business.

Paul's undoubted knowledge, experience and passion to help improve the accountant's role comes across in every chapter of this book."

Wayne Hockley, Director, Anthony Russel, Braintree, England

"I was inspired to be a Chartered Accountant by seeing what a business-savvy accountant called David did for my parents and their business. My parents worked hard, but the success of their business enabled me to enjoy a better life and certainly an upgrade on my holidays! They never made a major decision without David's input. He was their sounding board, corporate finance man and friend.

One summer in his office David showed me he had a team delivering numbers. A team that meant he could spend his time understanding the numbers, talking to clients and using them to bring greater success to his clients.

Firms need to understand that being just an accountant was never enough and now, in the world of cloud accounting, the need to demonstrate you add value is more important than ever.

This book won't make you into a business savvy accountant, but it will challenge everything you've learnt and done in the profession to date. And then show you how others have done it successfully so that you can follow their lead."

Vipul Sheth ACA CTA, Managing Director, Advance Track Outsourcing, England

"Inspiration comes first and that is exactly what Paul's book provides, along with his positive and realistic enthusiasm teamed with his refreshing energy to transform your accountancy practice into a more valuable one"

Zoe Lacey-Cooper, Event Director, Accountex, England

"This book tells you everything good about Paul Shrimpling's approach and contribution to the accountancy profession. Anyone who has seen him present would vouch that Paul can never be accused of being half-hearted, and this book oozes passion and wholehearted advice from the first page. The book is filled with straightforward and common-sense advice, and Paul's credibility comes not only from his thousands of hours one-to-one with accountants looking to improve their businesses but also his ability to get others to open up about the secrets of their success. This is a must-read for any accountant looking forward to the digital age with a little trepidation."

Douglas Aitken, CEO, Croner Business School, England

"Paul Shrimpling has done an awesome job of identifying what it takes to be a Business Growth Accountant and how important it is as accountants to embrace the change from compliance work to business advisory. Whilst it's easy to read, it's packed full of detailed information. This is essential reading if you want your accounting practice to thrive in the future."

Amanda Fisher, CFO and Mentor, amandafisher.com, Australia

"A lot of "Has Beans" style accountants are blindly burying their heads in the sand, blind to the fact that traditional accountancy work is rapidly disappearing out of their to do list. Paul's book provides a practical route map to a valuable way of delivering profitable advisory services to business clients."

Michael Ogilvie, Managing Director, OBC The Accountants, England

"For any firm that is looking at staying ahead of the inevitable 'march of automation', this is the book for you.

Sharing knowledge and facts is no longer the role of the advisor, Google will do that far better. Your ability to remain relevant in the new digital age will depend on your skills in questioning, building rapport and connecting with your clients at a far deeper level.

As machines get better at answering questions... you need to get better at asking them. Paul's book shows you just how to do that."

Alex Davis, Business Development, UK QuickBooks

"Paul's book is an invaluable guide to all those firms of accountants wanting to make themselves relevant to tomorrow's client needs; to grow and succeed in a world where technology means that the traditional accountant has little place or relevance."

Peter Taaffe, Managing Director, BWM Chartered Accountants, England

"Having worked with him for a number of years it's great to see Paul's book bring together superbly many insights into how an accountancy firm can address the core challenges now facing the profession.

In a constantly and now rapidly changing environment Paul shows how you can lay sound foundations on which to build a great accountancy practice.

This book is a must read for any practice that wants to grow, adapt and achieve its goals and will inspire you to do so"

Ian Rodgers, Managing Director, The Profit Key, England

12

"The effort, energy and passion that Paul has put into creating this go-to book for any serious accountant has been clear to see over the last year or so.

We meet with Paul every quarter and feel his inspiration! His enthusiasm transports itself across our team and fills us all with joy, anticipation and most importantly of all...drive. This is what the book does too. Paul's book is full of inspiring, yes, literally awe-inspiring thought and insight into how you can make your accountancy business a better business by helping your clients, by caring.

Top tip, once you have read the book, pick one thing, just one thing and do it...this will make you feel good and will encourage you to pick another one thing to do, before you know where you are you will have done lots! Small steps!"

Neil King, Managing Director, Cedar + Co, England

"If you want off the hamster wheel of endless tax returns for unappreciative clients, and if you want to make a real difference in the lives and businesses of your clients, read this book.

While there's plenty of buzz out there that accountants need to add advisory services to their firms, there aren't too many sources that actually demonstrate how to do that.

Based on real world examples of accountants and advisors from around the world who are doing this work and on Paul's years of experience guiding firms, this book lays out the steps you'll need to take to transform your firm into Business Growth Accountants."

Liz Farr, CPA, Farr Communications, New Mexico, USA

"Last year we felt under considerable pressure to add new fees. We met with Paul in March, agreed a weekly plan of action and in 9 months scored a major goal for the firm, adding £327,000 in new fees."

– Neil Driver, Davis Grant Chartered Accountants,
Ilford, England

The Business Growth Accountant *is a game-changer for the accounting profession. It's a 'call to arms' for accountants everywhere to move from the 'bean-counter' to the strategic trusted advisor.*

Technology is inexorably advancing client expectations and redefining what they deem to be of value. To get ahead of the game, Paul Shrimpling's Higher Value Route Map is a powerful framework that charts the optimal path for accountants to be the difference makers needed by today's business owners. A terrific 3-hour read and a must for forward thinking accountants throughout the world."

Rob Brown, Host of the "Top 100 Club Accounting"
Podcast, Author of Build Your Reputation and
Founder of the BD Academy, England

"I worked with Paul for a number of years. He was coach, consultant, adviser, friend and trusted aide all at the same time. Paul's knowledge, experience and expertise of the accountancy profession is simply brilliant.

He helped transform our firm and I'm forever indebted to him for all his support. I'm thrilled that Paul has written this book where he openly and transparently shares key insights into how to create an exceptional accountancy firm.

I think the book is a must-read for all accountants who are serious about running a remarkable practice."

Shaz Nawaz, ACA, Director, AA Accountants,
England

"I find it fascinating that since working with Paul we have reduced turnover but more than doubled profits. Our debt has vanished, and stress levels are under control. It's altogether a lot more fun."

– Neil King, Cedar & Co, Derby, England

"The thing about this sequence of meetings with Paul, and the follow-up calls, is that after only 3 months, the landscape looks much clearer for us all. It is almost as if, for the first time, we have had our heads lifted up, and we can see the opportunities for change which previously had been buried."

– Nick Price, EuraAudit, Harrogate, England

"Thank you for running what was a very productive marketing workshop with our ten Directors. I'm not sure we have ever received such a positive reaction from the whole group, and what made it even more satisfying for me was that the ones we thought would *be cynical were anything but!* A great achievement, which bodes well for the future."

– Laurie Riley , Dyke Yaxley Chartered, Accountants, Shrewsbury, England

"Paul spent an hour of his time at the conference giving me some extremely valuable tips. Several business coaches and business gurus had told me that I needed to increase my fees, but no-one could give me a step-by-step method on how to go about this and how to determine the "right" price."

– Jessica Pillow, Pillow May, Wiltshire, England

"I continue to be impressed by the energy and enthusiasm with which Paul challenges, inspires and guides our firm. Just speaking with Paul will renew enthusiasm for what's possible in your accountancy business."

– Clive Wilson, Landmark Chartered Accountants, Watford, England

"In the short time that I have worked with Paul, he has made a significantly positive impact on our accountancy business. Paul is extremely knowledgeable and his advice has been invaluable."

– Joe Sole, Sole Associates, Surrey, England

"Paul provides many answers to the mysteries of how to deliver advisory services in his book, The Business Growth Accountant.

Accounting professionals have been being told for years to be an advisor, with no real training on the path to get there. Paul provides the steps with his "Higher-Value Route Map" in his book, as well as, real life scenarios from experienced accountants that deliver advisory services from around the world.

This book will help you take the steps needed to be comfortable with the critical conversations that are necessary to be a truly value-added strategic partner to your client that they couldn't imagine living without."

– Amy Vetter, CPA.CITP, CGMA, Keynote Speaker, Advisor and Author of Integrative Advisory Services: Expanding Your Accounting Services Beyond the Cloud, USA

The Business Growth Accountant

Transform your accountancy practice into a profitable and valuable advisory business

Paul Shrimpling

"When you think about an accountant, what do you really think of? You think of someone who is an historian, accountants report on history.

But what if we turned that upside down and what if we said that what accountants actually do is, help clients create history."

Paul Dunn, B1G1

"Man-up and smash it"

Jake Shaw – 1993-2014

"I'm a card-carrying member of the Institute of Chartered Accountants, so you know, my biases are crystal clear. I remember the days – it might sound like I'm old, but – when a chartered accountant actually meant business advisor.

And that's what I like to see, where the word accountant is actually meaning business advisor."

Steve Major,

Chartered Accountant,

Business Advisor

...the words you speak and the numbers you talk about can change the lives of your business owner clients

...this book has been created to help you use the best words and use the best numbers

First Printing: 2018

Copyright © 2018 by Paul Shrimpling

Printed in the United Kingdom.

Contents

About the author

After 15 years of working exclusively with accountants in practice, Paul's passion and energy for the profession is as strong as ever.

Paul Shrimpling

Paul has conducted more than 1,100 one-on-one non-exec-style meetings with the owners and directors of both small and large accountancy firms.

Paul has presented to rooms full of accountants at events run by the ICAEW, ACCA, Accountex, Intuit, AVN, Thomson Reuters, Peak Performance, Futrli and others.

Paul also gets asked to run team away days and strategic retreats for accounting firms. In addition, he sometimes gets involved in presenting to the business-owner clients of accounting firms, to talk about the power and value of KPIs.

And every two months Paul creates a four-page Business Breakthrough report for accountants. Every report is short and easy-to-read and is written to inspire and educate accountants on a wide variety of business growth subjects. And now, more than 30 firms take 'Business Bitesize', brand it for themselves and distribute it to all their clients and contacts so that they too can inspire their business owners to grow.

About the contributors

This book exists because of the generosity of a host of accountants and industry commentators.

You'll find I have attributed their comments and quotes throughout the book so that you can apply your own judgement about the insights given.

My deepest thanks to you all:

Andrew Botham	Accrington, England	Owner Mayes Accountancy
		Founder of Business One Page Plan

http://bit.ly/2GGe78v

For the full link go visit

https://www.linkedin.com/in/andrew-botham-46271012/

Aynsley Damery	Cheltenham, UK	CEO of Tayabali Tomlin
		Co-founder of TaxGo

http://bit.ly/2G1icXh or for the full link visit:

https://www.linkedin.com/in/aynsleydamery/

| **Alex Davis** | London, UK | Business Development Manager, Intuit UK |

http://bit.ly/2DDpqeP or for the full link visit:

https://www.linkedin.com/in/alexldavis/

| **Hannah Dawson** | Brighton, UK | Founder, CEO of Futrli |

https://www.linkedin.com/in/hannah-dawson-8a3b2b15/

| **Paul Dunn** | Singapore | B1G1 Chairman |

Founder of Results Corporation – Boot Camp

http://bit.ly/2poHIv7 or for the full link visit:

https://www.linkedin.com/in/paulsdunn/

| **Amanda Fisher** | Sydney, Australia | CFO & Business Mentor |

Speaker & Author

http://bit.ly/2FSU8Cr or for the full link visit:

https://www.linkedin.com/in/amandafisherca/

Steph Hinds	Newcastle, Australia	Head Ninja and accountant at GrowthisWe
		Xero firm of the year 2012

http://bit.ly/2G2Ckbt or for the full link visit:

https://www.linkedin.com/in/growthwisesteph/

Paul Kennedy	Enfield, UK	Managing Director of O'Byrne & Kennedy Chartered Accountants
		VeraSage fellow

http://bit.ly/2FU3A8N or for the full link visit:

https://www.linkedin.com/in/paul-kennedy-641a721/

Steve Major	Australia	Founder of The Revolutionary Firm
		Founder of Pricing Power

http://bit.ly/2pngepG or for the full link visit:

https://www.linkedin.com/in/stevemajor21/

| **Ric Payne** | New South Wales, Australia | Thought Leader & Chairman of the Principa Group of Companies |
| | | President & CEO of Results Accountants' Systems |

http://bit.ly/2IBxS1R or for the full link visit:

https://www.linkedin.com/in/richard-payne-7890691/

| **Steve Pipe** | Leeds, UK | Speaker, strategist and Amazon 5 star rated business author |
| | | Founder of AVN |

http://bit.ly/2plUGdQ or for the full link visit:

https://www.linkedin.com/in/stevepipe/

| **Greg Smargiassi** | Perth, Australia | Founder and CEO of OURCFO |
| | | Educator teaching SMEs financial mastery |

http://bit.ly/2FUY5X8 or for the full link visit:

https://www.linkedin.com/in/gregsmargiassi/

Luke Smith   Jersey, UK   Founder of Purpose

Finance Director of
Repowering London

http://bit.ly/2GIFm2n or for the full link visit:

https://www.linkedin.com/in/lukesmithvfd/

James   Sydney,   Co-founder of Aptus
Solomons   Australia   Accounting and
Advisory

Head of Accounting
at Xero

http://bit.ly/2DHYsCQ or for the full link visit:

https://www.linkedin.com/in/jamessolomonsca/

Peter Taaffe   Liverpool, UK   Owner & MD of
BWMacfarlane
Chartered
Accountants

http://bit.ly/2tWcP6A or for the full link visit:

https://www.linkedin.com/in/peter-taaffe-1a8a3b1a/

| **Rob Walsh** | Wiltshire, UK | Owner and Managing Director of Clear Vision Accountancy Ltd |
| | | Specialist Business Consultant and Mentor |

http://bit.ly/2HKTmbg or for the full link visit:

https://www.linkedin.com/in/robwalsh1/

| **Nick Williams** | London, UK | National Business Development Manager |
| | | Specialist Business Consultant and Mentor |

http://bit.ly/2u5JneI or for the full link visit:

https://www.linkedin.com/in/nick-williams-661969/

Acknowledgments

Books are always a team effort.

Inspiration comes first... Mine comes from Rob Walsh, Steve Pipe, Paul Dunn, Ernest Oriente, Ron Baker and all the accountants I've been privileged to work with so far.

And a special mention for Jake Shaw who we watched grow up into a fabulous young man. Jake was unfortunately taken from us in a tragic accident when only 21, but Jake and his family continue to inspire me and my family. Life is for living, wholehearted, all in.

Then comes the graft... The Remarkable Practice team have grafted long and hard to make this book a reality. My wholehearted and heartfelt thanks to Nickie Shaw, Sherri Medcalf and, of course, Kate Shrimpling for getting the book over the line. And thank you also to Kelly Atherton and Sally Walwin for doing everything necessary to make sure the book got into your hands.

Christopher John Payne helped me get draft one over the line with his team, Farah, Ken and Naomi at Effort-Free Media.

Special mentions...

Rob Walsh, Simon Chaplin and Stephen Smallwood get a special mention because they backed me when I started Remarkable Practice back in 2007.

The team at Intuit get a big thank you for the trip to California to see the scale of the opportunity facing every accountancy firm on the planet, and for enabling several interviews and insights that show up in these pages.

And like the saying goes:

> *"If I have seen further than others, it is by standing on the shoulders of giants"*

Isaac Newton

I hope the ideas and insights you find in this book help you see further and help you make the most of the amazing opportunity facing the accountancy profession.

1

Why this book?

The day before Christmas Eve, when I was 20, my dad was fired from his high-powered production director job because of a heated argument with the business owner.

So, over Christmas, Dad decided to start his own upholstery business. His first call was to an accountant.

It was easy for me to ditch my mundane contracts engineer job with Lucas Aerospace and get involved, so I did. I soon sold the first piece of furniture to a retailer in Nottingham.

It was a slow start. Dad and I turned to each other when making decisions but, as I now know, we could have been more successful, more quickly.

One of the chairs we sold from our Chelsea showroom

Just like a golfer can't see her swing, we were too close to our business to make the best decisions.

Yes, we grew the business into a £1million turnover business. Yes, we exported to the USA, to the Middle East and to the home of stylish furniture, Scandinavia. We also opened a Chelsea Harbour showroom. We built our own custom-designed production premises too. But...

Business challenges are never far away!

Yes, we experienced cash flow challenges. We fought our way through two recessions. We got so close to failure that the insolvency firm recommended we call it a day. We refinanced the business and fought our way back. We got the business ready for sale. We saw the sale fall through because our team walked out and set up their own business supplying our previously loyal customers.

And yes, eventually, as well as the first piece of furniture, I had the honour of selling the last piece of furniture our company ever made.

These experiences were of our making, created by our decisions and our actions (or inaction). But we were too close to it all to make the best decisions.

Back then I just didn't know. But I know now. I know now because of the valuable guidance I get from my current accountant. I know we would have benefited from a finance-savvy guide, to hold our hand when it mattered, when the lumpy difficult decisions were being made.

Where was our accountant on this rocky road?

Our accountant was mostly noticeable by his absence.

What we got was a once-a-year discussion about a six-month-old set of annual accounts and the odd phone call (for which we were billed).

I should have known better, but I didn't. In one exceptional moment, our accountant did, however, recommend a pension expert who proved to be invaluable in setting up a healthy retirement fund for my parents.

No excuses!

I'm not making excuses; the results and difficulties we achieved were of our own making. I didn't seek out a better accountant, so we got the accountant we deserved.

At the time, I didn't know that I could have found a helpful, valuable and caring *Business Growth Accountant*.

What do YOUR business-owner clients deserve?

Don't your business-owner clients deserve to have a trusted advisor 'watching their swing', influencing their thinking, influencing their decisions and influencing their actions?

Luke Skywalker discovered 'the force' thanks to Obi-Wan Kenobi!

Andy Murray started winning majors when he hooked up with Ivan Lendl and his fitness team.

At Remarkable Practice, I have Rob, Ernest and Neil. Two of them are accountants. All three have influenced, helped focus, inspired and influenced the changes at Remarkable Practice.

My experiences conclusively prove that all business owners deserve to have a guide, a support, a challenger, a sounding board. And when such a guide is 'numbers savvy', all the better.

And because your business clients trust you, their accountant, you are the best chance they have of improving their business thinking. When you commit to constructive conversations to help them improve their thinking, you'll improve their decision-making. Improve their decision-making and you'll improve the actions they take. Improve the actions they take and their results will improve, too.

Please get stuck in

See your clients more often.

Ask them the obvious questions *and* the difficult questions so that they improve their thinking, improve their behaviour and improve their results.

Be there for your clients on their rocky road, when it matters. Which, in my experience, is more often than you think.

The ideas, insights, skills and habits shared in this book are designed to help and support you.

2

Worldwide change for good

"If you don't like change, you're going to like irrelevance even less."

General Eric Shinseki

The world is changing...

The accountant's world is changing fast.

And as a profession, as a community, accountants can play an important role in changing the world – one accountancy firm and one business owner at a time.

Some accountants (several provide the inspiration for this book) already help change the lives of their business-owner clients.

You can do more of the same.

If you have the will to make a difference to your business-owner clients, then you can change the world of your business-owner clients.

This book has been created to inspire, challenge and encourage you.[1]

I know this is stating the blindingly obvious but...

...all of your clients are connected to your firm.

It's a unique and powerful relationship.

It's this unique and powerful relationship that places you and your firm in a position of power, influence and authority.

Every accountancy firm across the globe, including yours, has an opportunity to profoundly influence the results of its business-owner clients.

---

[1] *Working with Simon Chaplin at GreenStones for several years was an education in itself. While working with him on the values of the firm, Simon coined the phrase 'inspire, challenge and support', which underpins everything GreenStones stands for. So, I've borrowed a little of Simon's genius and I hope this book does inspire, challenge and encourage you too.*

And so, as a profession, the opportunity to have a global impact is significant and should not be ignored – one accountancy firm at a time, one business owner at a time.

But so many accountants and accountancy firms fail to grasp the opportunity to make a big difference.

This book has been created to help you and your firm grasp the opportunity and make a difference.

But there's a problem looming...

Trust is imploding

One of the most recognised commentators on trust is the Edelman Trust Barometer[2].

The 2017 report shows a dropping of trust across all walks of life.

Richard Edelman calls it *"an implosion of trust"* which suggests that any accountant taking for granted their position as a 'trusted advisor' is running the risk of losing that trust.

Pointing to a solution Edelman suggests:

> *"...the three most important attributes for building trust are treating employees well,*

---

[2] *https://www.edelman.com/executive-summary/*

For the shortened url visit http://bit.ly/2HOraV4

> *offering high quality products and services, and listening to customers."*

The centrepiece of this book is the conversation you have with each and every client.

The backbone of every valuable conversation is the art and science of asking questions and listening.

The art and science of asking questions featured in every one of the interviews with every Business Growth Accountant included in this book.

Sea-change is unavoidable

You don't need to ask any questions to see the sea-change facing all businesses, especially accountancy businesses.

Your business-owner clients are increasingly using technology to help their business succeed.

In the UK, Xero added 120,000 new customers to the 133,000 they reported in 2016. Intuit are adding new customers just as fast and at the time of writing had 166,000 QuickBooks Online (QBO) users in the UK.

Throw Artificial Intelligence (AI), Machine Learning and Big Data into the technology melting pot, and the changes are going to be even greater. Globally, cloud accounting is transforming the accountancy business and accountancy landscape.

Cloud accounting is now part of the accounting landscape and it's only going to get smarter, faster and more useful to your business owner clients.

Is this technology sea-change unavoidable?

It pays to ask yourself: is cloud accounting just another piece of tech or is it a fundamental shift for the accounting profession?

A recent visit to the Californian HQ of Intuit proved to be educational about the scale and speed of change hitting the accountancy and business communities.

The QBConnect conference the following day also proved the power of technology. Having done software demos from stage myself, I appreciated the terror (and confidence in the tech) of proving that voice recognition plus QBO, plus a dose of AI works. And it works now. It worked in front of an audience of 5,000+.

It worked, showing how a business owner can ask QuickBooks Assistant (on the Apple iPhone or Android), how this month's business bank balance compares with the bank balance from the same month last year. Further questions generate more insights into cost comparisons. And when the results also compare benchmarked results from other similar businesses, the value of the technology shines through even more.

This (bravely-done) demo was only a signpost of soon-to-be available technology for your business-owner clients. But there was more.

When AI can identify a shortage of cash in a business, can identify how strong the fundamentals of the business finances are, and then offer the business owner a loan within QBO, the tech proves its value at an even deeper level. QuickBooks Capital is Intuit's business lending facility and has been testing this with businesses in the USA.

Technology is changing fast.

And the rate of technology change is getting faster.

As you can see, it's getting more valuable too.

What you're up against?

1. Your competition

2. Your old ways holding you back

3. Changing expectations of your business-owner clients

Can your competition influence your behaviour?

If an accounting firm like Armstrong Watson (multi-partner, multi-office, multi-million-pound firm) can transition 4,500 clients onto Xero in a year (that's almost 100 businesses a week!) then you know what's possible and you know what you're up against too.

And if you were starting an accounting business from new, you would only work with cloud accounting. All the younger accounting firms I come across are 'cloud-accounting-only' firms.

Your immediate challenge is that desktop-based accounting still works and is still used. This makes it easy to take cloud adoption slowly. It also makes it easy to think the cloud is just another bit of tech rather than a fundamental shift.

Do you want your old ways of working to undermine your firm's future? Do you want to allow your competition to get a march on you? Do you want to ignore the increasing expectations of your clients?

I think not. And so action is needed.

Half pregnant?

Technology is making your accountancy business either more relevant and valuable to your clients or it's making you and your firm totally irrelevant.

There's no halfway house on this.

Like my friend Steve Pipe says:

"...you can't be half pregnant!"

I often ask audiences of accountants whether they think the **rate of change** in the profession is slowing down, staying the same or getting faster.

Well, how would you answer?

All the evidence points to the rate of change getting faster. Much faster. Exponentially faster.

This increasing rate of change is technology driven.

Moore's Law predicts a two-fold increase in computing power every two years. And over the last 40+ years Moore's Law has been seen to happen apparently without end.[3]

That's a doubling of computing power 20 times.

And if you double anything 20 times it's going to have an exponential impact.

If you have any doubt about the power of such a doubling check out these two stories about golf and scaling Everest...

---

[3] *Moore's Law has proved true for decades longer than its originator, Gordon Moore, predicted. The end of Moore's Law is being predicted again. However, seven technologies in development suggest that the end of Moore's Law is far from over. If you want to know more, check out this video to see what's coming:* http://bit.ly/2hq2NC2. *There's evidence to suggest Moore's Law is far from over when you read this article by a tech analyst backing a claim from Intel:* http://bit.ly/2nrmSIi

Paper-fold to Everest

The world record for folding a piece of paper is 12 times[4].

But if you could fold a (large enough) piece of paper 27 times, how thick would it be?

Fold a piece of paper 27 times and the pile of paper will be higher than Everest!

Get to 42 folds – 42 doublings – and you're at the moon![5]

Moore's law has seen 20 doublings of computing power.

Because of this exponential improvement in technology, artificial intelligence, machine learning and big data are here now.

Intuit is now lending money to businesses through QuickBooks Capital, which is available through QuickBooks Online (QBO). This works because Intuit's big data and machine learning processes enable them to

---

[4] *Britney Gallivan, in 2002, demonstrated that a piece of (toilet) paper 1220 metres long can be folded 12 times - contradicting the general acceptance that the limit is 6 or 7 folds.*

[5] *2 to the power of 42 applied to the thickness of a sheet of paper is greater than the distance to the moon.* http://www.codersrevolution.com/blog/will-a-piece-of-paper-folded-42-times-reach-the-moon

For the shortened url visit http://bit.ly/2G3lPf5

quickly and easily identify businesses with a minimum credit risk and a high likelihood of success. When algorithms identify a good lending prospect the business owner is notified within their QBO app that borrowing is available to them, almost instantly. This is live in the USA already.

Can you afford to watch the technology pass you by?

Kodak sat and watched its competitors adopt digital technology, which led to the death of Kodak.

Even though Kodak invented the digital camera.

Even though Kodak held a near-monopoly in the camera-film world (it pays not to be tied to desktop computing).

The advance of technology is transforming the legal profession too, and the health profession (IBM's Big Blue is a better judge of cancers and treatments than the best of Harley Street!).

What chance for a stuck-in-the-mud accountant?

All the evidence points to the rate of change in the accounting profession getting faster. Much faster.

You, your team, your firm, must either embrace the change or run the risk of repeating the Kodak story.

Put your clients front and central and embrace new technology wholeheartedly, and you'll set yourself up for success and will avoid becoming the next Kodak.

A £1 bet doubled over 18 holes?

You'd be wise not to 'try this at home'!

Bet £1 on hole 1 of an 18-hole golf course and agree to double the bet every hole thereafter.

How much do you end up betting on hole 18?

£2 on hole 2.

£4 bet on hole 3. £8 bet on hole 4. And so on.

You'll be betting a lumpy sum on hole 18...

£131,072

Moore's law has delivered 20 doublings of computing power and memory in the last 40 years. IF there were 20 holes on a golf course the bet would be up to £524,288. All from an initial £1 bet at hole 1.

And the next technology doubling is happening. Ignoring the technology will make your firm irrelevant.

> *"If you don't like change, you're going to like irrelevance even less."*

> *General Eric Shinseki*

Change or irrelevance is a choice, your choice.

Embracing cloud accounting is not optional, it's crucial to your firm's future (please don't repeat the Kodak story).

But it's not just about the technology it's about purpose – what's yours?

From 'must do' to 'want to'

You'll hear from accountancy firms in this book that are driven to help their clients succeed. It is crystal clear to these firms why they are doing what they are doing.

You'll also hear how these firms start from different places, they have different motivators that got them started in a business growth accountants role.

So, what's motivating you to get started or advance your firm's advisory work? What's driving you? In other words, what's your purpose?

There are many researchers, commentators, authors and philosophers who'll give you guidance on motivation and purpose – from Maslow (and his hierarchy of needs[6]) to more contemporary commentators like Simon Sinek (in his book 'Start With Why'[7]).

For speed and ease see which one (or more of) of these drivers gets your juices flowing:

---

[6] *Maslow's hierarchy of needs*

[7] *Check out this Ted talk by Simon Sinek for a 15 minute masterclass on the importance of getting clear on your reason for being in business*

Purpose – your desire to do worthwhile and meaningful work

Relatedness – your desire to be connected and interact with others

Autonomy – your desire to be in control of your work and your future

Mastery – your desire to get better and better at what you do

Status – your desire to maintain or improve your position be seen as valuable and valued

Fairness – your desire to work in a meritocracy where everyone is respected

This list is not definitive but does capture a strong cross-section of the major motivators of the human race – feel free to add any other(s) that motivate you.

Another way of working out what drives you, using this list, is to see what winds you up, frustrates you or hacks you off when each one of these drivers are reduced or threatened.

The business advisory firms interviewed for this book consistently demonstrated a desire for mastery – they want to advance their knowledge, skill and insights. They also have a deep, genuine desire to make a difference with their business owner clients.

And this desire to make a difference often extends beyond the business owners to making a difference in their communities and wider society too.

It's this stretch to make a difference to wider society that also drives me and my team to participate in the works you can find

Some of the firms interviewed here contribute

As a B1G1 Business For Good, we at Remarkable Practice incorporate purpose and meaning to our business through giving.

Buying this book means that together we are making great difference improving food production for a village by sponsoring the costs to build irrigation systems for community fruit and vegetable gardens for one year. Your support will help to generate year-round food and income.

3

Death of the 'bean counter'?

Alan Cowperthwaite of Harvey Smith Chartered Accountants in Essex talks heatedly about the way business owners refer to accountants as 'bean counters'.

Alan hates the 'bean counter' phrase!

Quite rightly, Alan takes responsibility for changing his clients' perspective so that they see him and his firm as so much more than 'bean counters'.

But could we now be seeing the end of the bean counter altogether? Or at least the start of the end?!

Leaving behind the bean counter terminology requires a big change.

And radical change is here, now.

Cloud accounting, machine learning, artificial intelligence and big data all add the radical change you're facing. Government initiatives for quarterly reporting (*Making Tax Digital in the UK*) helps force the use of greater technology and will result in technology replacing much of the work accountants and bookkeepers do now.

We've yet to see the full impact of these technologies, but they are coming like a train. A rather fast train!

Plus, we've yet to see the impact of block chain, virtual reality and many other technologies just leaving the drawing board.

Even with the technology currently in use, the value of your firm is being eroded, unless you're putting the technology to work in your firm in a radical way.

Your firm's capital value is threatened

These big changes bring into question the capital value of a traditional accountancy firm.

The 1 x GRF (gross recurring fees) model has been around for many decades. And the 1 x GRF model has been a cornerstone for the retirement funds of most partner/owners of accounting firms.

But how can 1 x GRF hold firm when desktop accounting packages are being seriously challenged by cloud accounting? Or when annual accounts are being challenged by quarterly reporting?

Who would want to invest a large sum into a firm that is stuck in the old annual accounts, desktop accounting and reporting 7 or more months after the client's year end?

In the light of the new ways in which many firms are working, the 1 x GRF model seriously over-values firms which are stuck in the old ways of working.

Perhaps the 1 x GRF model has life for firms who successfully transition clients from annual accounts to the instant reporting that cloud accounting enables.

Similarly, it won't be long before your business-owner clients expect the instant reporting that cloud accounting now makes available to them. In the UK, it will soon be a requirement, thanks to the government's Making Tax Digital initiative.

Yes, client expectations are changing, but what remains firm are the feelings business owners want to experience about their accountant. Confidence, certainty, reassured.

Your clients' expectations are substantially connected to the 'F' word.

It's mostly about the 'F' word!

As much as your training as an accountant would suggest that measurable results are the most important factor, the numbers AREN'T what matters most.

Try this on for size...

...it will be the way your client FEELS as a result of your involvement that will stick in the memory (the 'F' word is Feeling).

Four key results for your firm

Yes, the measurable outcomes play a vital role, but ultimately the way your client FEELS about you and your firm dictates four key results:

1. Client loyalty

2. Willingness to buy more from you

3. Willingness to recommend you and your firm

4. Willingness to pay you more for what you do

All four outcomes improve or decline depending on how you, your team and the work you do make a client feel about you and your firm.

Your client can feel good enough to recommend you, to buy more or to pay more even if the impact, the result or the outcome of the work you do is lower than either of you would like.

It's your ***client's perception of value*** that matters most.

Your client's perception of value is connected most significantly with the way they feel about you and your firm.

The results you help them achieve influences their feelings, for sure. But...

...just as the price you charge matters less than the way that you price (your pricing process[8])...

...what you do matters less than the way that you do it!

As Fun Boy Three and Bananarama sang in the '80s!

> *"It ain't what you do it's the way that you do it...*
>
> *...and that's what gets results!"*

As Ron Baker[9] suggested at a recent QuickBooks conference to hundreds of accountants:

> *"Value is not a number, it's a feeling"*

---

[8] *You'll find much more on pricing business growth accountancy later in chapter 11.*

[9] *Ron Baker (co-author with Paul Dunn of the book 'Firm Of The Future) was presenting a breakout session on 'the end of cost accounting' at the San Jose QuickBooks Connect conference and in a discussion around value pricing (on which he is a world-renowned expert) touched on the true meaning of value – client feelings.*

When you've just enjoyed a lovely meal in a lovely restaurant with lovely service, you'll express the value you received as a feeling.

Whether it be driving a new car or being looked after in a hotel or receiving exceptional client care from your computer service engineer, all generate a feeling.

Accountants and Business Growth Accountants do the same, and the potential for changing a business's results can generate large, deep and long-lasting feelings.

Hence Ron Baker's comment:

"Value is not a number, it's a feeling"

When you accept that true value is a feeling (not a number), a couple of questions present themselves:

1. What feelings do you want clients to experience thanks to your involvement?

2. Where and when do you have the biggest impact on your client's feelings?

You can see Aynsley Damery's focus on feelings when he shares the tone of the conversations he and his team have with business owners:

> *"We're asking them what they're feeling, what their concerns are. We're telling them that we know or demonstrating that we clearly know those are concerns and that we clearly can help*

> *them overcome them and that just by talking*
> *differently, people automatically open (up)."*

Later in our conversation Aysnley shares his customer focus for the products and services they develop and deliver at Tayabali Tomlin:

> *"...we have identified the pains of business*
> *owners and we've tried to introduce services and*
> *products, to deliver them to clients to try and*
> *overcome their pains."*

Aynsley wants to take away the painful feelings of running a business.

A bank wins by appealing to feelings...

It can be hard to see the tangible commercial value of feelings – it can 'feel' a bit pink and fluffy!

But an article in the Harvard Business Review[10] by Magids, Zorfas and Leemon points to the commercial power of emotions.

---

[10] *This HBR article delves into the science and value of emotions and how to influence emotions for a financial payoff* *https://hbr.org/2015/11/the-new-science-of-customer-emotions#comment-section or http://bit.ly/2GI8cQx*

The authors describe how, after a major bank introduced a credit card for Millennials that was designed to inspire emotional connection, use among the segment increased by **70%** and new account growth rose by **40%**.

What would you give for new client growth of 40% and possible cross sales of 70%?

Want to grow your firm's fees? Answer the two questions posed above and help your team see connections between the work they do and your clients' feelings.

Develop a much deeper relationship with your business-owner clients and it should be easier and far more valuable for you to appeal to your business owners' feelings.

Putting feelings to work for you and your firm

So, your client's feelings matter more than the numbers.

As a business growth accountant, should you be focused on the numbers or on the feelings the numbers generate?

Yes, numbers will generate feelings!

Share a net profit figure with a business-owner client and the number will generate a feeling of 'elation' or 'disappointment' or, possibly, 'disinterest'.

But isn't it the change in the numbers that's the source of their feeling? Net profit that goes from 'bad to worse' or from 'bad to good' or from 'good to great' will profoundly influence a business owner's emotional response.

When describing the skills that deliver value to business owners Hannah from Futrli points to a key but simple question set using this 'compare and contrast' insight:

> *"How have you done since the last time I saw you? How are we tracking progress?*

Numbers are relative. Net profit is compared with last year's net profit or the forecast or desired net profit. The value you deliver to your business-owner client (the feelings they experience) comes from the comparison. It's the comparison that creates the feeling.

You deliver greater value (better feelings) when you help a business owner improve their numbers.

Later in the book we talk about the power of questions. Use questions to discover what comparisons your clients are making. And then find out how they feel about them. This will be a source of meaningful and valuable conversation.

Just keeping score is emotionally bland

Most accountants help business owners keep score, like any good bean counter would.

Business Growth Accountants are much more involved.

In any sports game the people keeping score aren't really connected to the action. It's the players and coaches that experience all the visceral feelings (value).

Business Growth Accountants aren't players in the day-to-day business with their clients, but they are very much partnering as a coach, mentor and sounding board.

Business Growth Accountants influence the numbers by influencing the conversations and the decisions made, as well as the actions taken. Better conversations, better decisions and better actions generate better results and, as a result, better, stronger feelings too. The value delivered when you move from keeping score to playing a role in the decision-making is far greater than simply keeping score.

Small accountancy firms with average fees of £20,000 or £30,000 or more are not just keeping score.

Sure, you can advance your 'keeping score' skills by moving from providing data processing to providing business intelligence. And this has value and delivers some stronger feelings for your business owners.

But get into conversation with business owners about goals, challenges, robust systems, KPIs and more, and you're entering the emotional playing field. You're influencing the way your business owner thinks, what they decide and what action they take. The emotional stakes are higher.

Before we get too deep into influencing the numbers, let's deal with two competing ways of keeping score.

The old way and the new way...

Old news is worthless

It's possible your firm is still rooted in the 20th century approach to accounts production – accounts once a year, presented several months after the client's year end date, using data from a desktop accounting software package (or worse!).

But what's the value of sharing old news?

What feelings does a report that is six months out-of-date generate in a business owner?

Keeping score is one thing. But keeping score when the score is six, seven, eight or even nine months out of date is verging on worthless. Most business owners will not care about old (but accurate) financial reports of the last financial year of their business, six months or more after it's over. Business owners care about this month, this week or today.

Annual reports may be enough for Companies House. But they are of little value to your business owners except for keeping them compliant in the eyes of the authorities, which is, of course, necessary and expected, if indeed not taken for granted.

The death of annual accounts

The value of annual accounts looks even worse when compared to the up-to-date alternative.

With QuickBooks, Xero and other cloud accounting packages, bank feeds and products like Receipt Bank and

Futrli, your firm is now able to share business intelligence 'as it happens'. And remember, you don't work in a bubble, your competition can now do this too.

In the light of cloud accounting and well-timed reporting, the old 20th century annual accounts model looks like it's past its sell-by date, maybe even dead-in-the-water! Yes, it's necessary for Companies House and HMRC requirements, but its perceived value by your clients is, at best, being seriously eroded. At worst, annual accounts are almost totally irrelevant to an up-to-date cloud accounting business.

The history of accountancy shows an understandable obsession with historical data processing, understandable because of the lack of access to the business results until the client releases their financial books and records (or Sage file).

Not anymore.

If you're still tied to the old 20th century annual accounts methodology(including desktop accounting software), your capital value is being eroded by the firms already embracing cloud accounting and new ways of delivering value (stronger feelings) to business owners.

Build greater capital value for your firm

The capital value of your firm ultimately depends on the amount another firm is willing to pay for it, or the amount your management team is willing to pay for it.

To take this one step further, when the day comes that you want to sell, the value of your firm will be determined by the number of firms or individuals bidding to buy it. The greater the number of bidders, the higher the price you'll get.

Ebay, car auctions and property auctions confirm this.

So, what does your firm have to do to attract multiple bidders?

Priority 1 is client loyalty

If you have a high client churn, you'll look like a higher-risk purchase and will therefore attract fewer, and probably lower, bidders.

After all, client loyalty is a good indicator of future fees and profits. Client loyalty will likely lead to cross sales, referrals and a willingness to pay more.

Your client's perceived value is everything

A client's willingness to stay loyal, to continue paying you, to refer you and to buy more from you is determined by the perceived value they get from you and your firm.

This may be stating the blindingly obvious, but value is a relative term. Value is determined by comparison with other purchases, or with possible purchases.

Comparisons of what exactly?

- Compare the value of annual accounts presented 6 or more months after the year end with the value of quarterly reports a week or two after the quarter end.

- Compare weekly bookkeeping updates with minimum interruption with an annual bookkeeping tidy-up involving lots of time-consuming, hassle-heavy queries and searches for missing receipts and invoices.

If the price for the two services is similar, perceived value for the well-timed quarterly reporting will be much higher than for the ancient history of your annual accounts service.

Even if quarterly reporting is more expensive than annual reporting, it could well be seen as being of higher value by most of your clients (or at least a healthy percentage of them). You have an opportunity to earn more because you're delivering more value (stronger feelings).

But what if you could give your business-owner clients additional, more emotionally-packed service levels to compare?

Time to step up to higher-value

You and your firm need to make a decision about the level of value you want to deliver to your clients.

Your business owners' expectations about quarterly reporting, monthly reporting, weekly reporting and even daily reporting is changing.

The UK Government's Making Tax Digital (MTD) initiative is making quarterly reporting non-negotiable.

What an opportunity you have!

But even without MTD, almost all your business clients have a mobile phone and a computer. Your clients already are, or will be, making more of the readily available cloud accounting products and apps. So, you either choose to be at the forefront of the adoption of cloud accounting and quarterly reporting, or behind it.

Providing well-timed data processing and quarterly reporting will be the bare minimum your clients will need from you.

Chances are you'll be doing more work and will need to charge higher fees.

Chances are your clients will resist higher prices.

So, it pays to share higher-value options for clients to compare with your new, but necessary, quarterly reporting service.

To help you share higher-value service comparisons with your clients use the 'Higher-Value Route Map'[11] below...

---

[11] *For a full-colour A4 printable PDF of the 'Higher-Value Route Map' go to www.paulshrimpling.com/bga-resources. You can also get your hands on a PowerPoint version which enables you to*

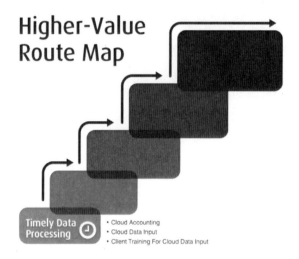

NB. The first level of the route map starts with 'timely data processing' rather than 'quarterly data processing' because some of your clients will demand monthly, weekly or even daily reporting.

Because of the advancement of technology plus the changing expectations of your clients, adopting cloud accounting is necessary and inevitable. It's also a big win for your firm and your client.

_____

present the layers to colleagues (and clients too). For the shortened url visit http://bit.ly/2plWsea

As Hannah Dawson from Futrli suggests:

> *"...an entrepreneur would much rather have 90% accuracy over information today than 100% in four weeks' time."*

Timely access to what's going on in their business will be valued by your business owner clients.

Resist the use of (cloud) technology or avoid it whilst your competition are embracing it and you'll be making your firm valueless to your clients and to any future buyer as well. Being a late adopter or laggard will make your firm irrelevant to ambitious, go-ahead, technology-savvy business owners.

However, being at the forefront of promoting and delivering new technology solutions for your business owners will set you up for long term survival and success.

Timely data processing won't be enough

Bear in mind that Level 1, shown above, will soon be a technology-only commodity service.

Timely data processing if done in isolation however, will make it tough to justify profitable fee levels for your firm. A business owner will need less and less from an accountant for timely data processing – the technology will do more and more of this work. So...

...it makes sense to move up the 'Higher-Value Route Map' by changing the conversation with clients so that ***clients see and experience greater value from you and your firm***.

More value from Business Intelligence

Raw financial data about a business, even if it is well-timed, can be less than helpful.

Raw data can confuse, concern and even create conflict with your business owners.

You are the numbers experts, not them. So, shouldn't you help them interpret the raw data?

Yes, there's greater value in the interpretation.

And when we talked to Andrew Botham, whose £1.4million-firm annually generates fees of around £300,000 from 25 advisory clients, he asserted that there's massive value in limiting the amount of data clients see:

> *"...some of the biggest uplifts people have had are when we only track three measures. Because we've really identified what really is a game changer."*

Andrew's experiences prove that 'less really is more'.

Your job as the numbers expert is to interpret, filter and pre-select the numbers that will help your business-owner client and not to leave them to fend for themselves in a swamp of raw data.

Like Steph Hinds of GrowthWise suggests:

> *"...as accountants we are actually trained to analyse data... we do have a great analytical mind...*
>
> *...and data is just coming to us now really, really quickly and really easily and that's exciting."*

Your job is to provide a limited selection of useful and well-timed business intelligence, not a flood of timely data that the business owner is likely to ignore in the maelstrom and confusion of running their business.

> *"...your job as an accountant in that advisory space is not to complicate it, but to simplify it. Simplify, simplify, and part of that is to also make it visually attractive, so that it's easier for the business owner to interpret it.*
>
> *Your value as an accountant is in your interpretation skills."*

> *Hannah Dawson, Founder of Futrli*

Your job is to take the flood of well-timed data and help your client see the wood from the trees.

You've got this nearly real-time instant access to relevant business data. You've got an accountant's analytical approach. And you can easily unpick and identify the information from the data that's relevant to the business owner, data that might signpost the problem that they're looking to fix.

Your business owners will see greater value in this well-timed business intelligence and insight...

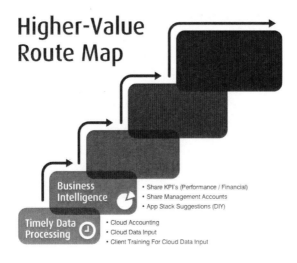

Real-time or well-timed?

Even with business intelligence I hesitate to use the phrase 'real-time' as most business owners will be happy with weekly or monthly business intelligence. A few would welcome daily reports – restaurants and bars and retail being obvious candidates.

The two key questions for each of your clients is what would be 'well-timed' for them and what 'business intelligence' will help them make better decisions.

Numbers that have no (or very little) relevance or influence on the business decisions of today are of little value to a business owner (although Companies House and HMRC seem to value them – but you don't work for HMRC you work for your clients!). This approach is what has earned the profession the 'bean counter' label which Alan Cowperthwaite detests so much.

Generally, accountants have historically worked with old numbers. Forecasts are a rarity in most accounting firms. And though management accounts are typically reporting on a more recent past, they rarely influence decisions as accountants largely just share the *numbers* with the business owner; they don't stimulate a **'constructive conversation'** about the forecast or the management accounts.

In a heated discussion about bean counters, Alan came up with a new phrase to reflect this needed change:

"From Has Beans to Magic Beans!"

From 'Has Beans' to 'Magic Beans'!

'Has Beans' are the old numbers from annual accounts of yesteryear!

'Has Beans' might also be used to describe accountants who resist, or just simply delay, the adoption of the cloud technology transforming the accountancy profession.

On the other hand, what are the 'Magic Beans' in which your business owners are really interested?

The Big 5 key financials that the business owners truly care about are:

1. Profit growth

2. Capital value growth

3. Cash flow improvement

4. Personal net worth increase

5. Less reliance (time) on the business owner

Are there really enough conversations taking place about these four numbers between your firm's people and your clients?

These four numbers are outcomes of a healthy business and ultimately reflect the success of your business clients.

If, and when, you prove to a business owner that you can help them positively improve these four numbers, you'll find it easy to demonstrate that you've delivered real value.

Your reputation for growing these four numbers will result in referrals and will result in you winning new high-value business-owner clients. Cross-selling additional services to your clients will be easier and your clients' willingness to pay you more will be a given.

These numbers have always been within the remit of the accountant. They are valuable, they generate strong feelings and should be part of your conversation but...

...for Business Intelligence to pay off you need to have more constructive conversations. Conversations that build value for your client.

The numbers on their own are not enough – even when they are the best, most relevant 'magic beans' numbers.

Talking builds growth and value

All the reporting in the world is of little value without a conversation that pulls out the important issues and opportunities.

Your role as a Business Growth Accountant has more to do with the value of the conversations you have than with the financial reports you provide.

It's one thing to have a conversation about the outcome measures – the results of doing great work.

It's even more powerful, meaningful and valuable to have conversations about the ***predictive numbers*** – the numbers that drive the future success of the business.

Typically predictive numbers are non-financial numbers (and you're the numbers expert remember). IT's these non-pedictive numbers that drive the success of a business. For example, when customer feedback numbers get worse they predict a declining business; when customer response times or quality measures improve client loyalty and sales revenue improves.

It pays to talk about the predictive drivers that generate the Big 4 outcomes of profit growth, capital value growth, cash flow improvement and personal net worth increase.

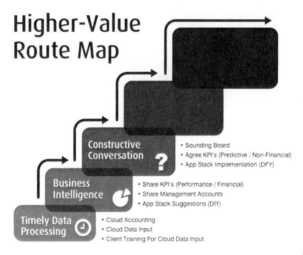

The Big 5 outcome numbers are not really the 'magic beans' - they are more like the gold pieces Jack (from Jack and the Beanstalk) collects from the giant's castle.

The Big 5 are the results, the outcomes, the key performance indicators (KPIs) of the work you do with your client.

The magic beans are different numbers, different measures, a different type of KPI.

The magic beans are the **Key Predictive Indicators** – the numbers (mostly non-financial) that signpost the actions needed to achieve the Big 4 outcomes for your business-owner client.

Chapter 9 goes into much more detail around the knowledge and skills needed to talk Key Predictive Indicators.

When you talk about the predictive non-financial numbers that drive business success, you deliver value to your client.

The value comes from a sense of confidence and certainty that the future looks bright, positive and successful.

Can you see how your role and reputation as the numbers expert can create ***constructive conversations*** that deliver massive client value? Value that earns you the right to charge more, just like the firms interviewed for this book charge more (upwards of £35,000 per client in one case).

More value from constructive conversations

Filtering **business intelligence**, on behalf of your client, from the flood of timely data is surely valuable, but not as valuable as holding a **conversation** to help your client see the value in the business intelligence numbers.

Step up the 'Higher-Value Route Map' from timely data to filtered business intelligence and then talk it through with your client. You'll be head and shoulders above most accountants and most accountancy firms.

It is the constructive conversations that will impress clients, helping them improve both their results and the way they feel about you and your firm. You'll have a competitive advantage.

But you can go further and have an even bigger impact on the results your clients achieve and the feelings they have for you and your firm.

What if you help, encourage and prompt your clients to make decisions?

Even more value from Deliberate Decisions

Meaningful and worthwhile conversations that help your business-owner client make deliberate decisions will be seen as substantially more valuable by your client.

> *"...entrepreneurs or managing directors or those in charge of the finance function just want to be able to make decisions today.*
>
> *They want to be able to make decisions today with the most up-to-date information they have, and to be able to look ahead at future decisions that they might need to make."*
>
> *Hannah Dawson, founder of Futrli*

Go and see your client (or at least call them) more often, and alert, explain and educate them (have a constructive conversation) about what the business intelligence is saying about their business. Then help them, guide them and even gently cajole them to make a deliberate decision to move their business forward.

Decisions your clients make from good, well-timed and filtered business intelligence are more likely to contribute to the success of their business.

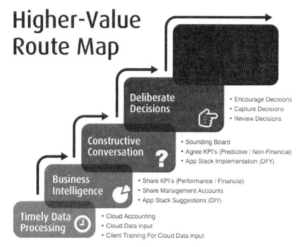

As the old adage goes:

> *"In any moment of decision, the best thing you can do is the right thing, the next best thing is the wrong thing, and the worst thing you can do is nothing."*
>
> *Theodore Roosevelt*

Use the good, well-timed and filtered business intelligence to educate your client. Then help them make a deliberate decision to advance their business.

Ultimately, a constructive conversation that results in a 'nice chat' but no decision does not contribute to the five big wins your business owners want:

1.   Profit growth

2.   Capital value growth

3.   Cash flow improvement

4.   Personal net worth increase

5.   Less reliance (time) on the business owner

Only by making decisions will change happen and improvements result.

Why not see your role as one of helping business owners make deliberate decisions towards their goals?

The science of great decision-making

Clearly there's risk attached to decision-making for your client.

Clearly there's risk attached to not making a decision too.

Your firm's good, well-timed and filtered business intelligence gives your client tangible, measurable and worthy-of-attention insights, on which to make a good decision.

The decision is ultimately one your client has to make, not you. But you deliver greater value when you help, encourage and prompt your client to make a decision.

You elevate the value of your constructive conversations when your client makes a decision.

Your skill at asking constructive questions helps you step up to this higher level of perceived value (and higher levels of feelings for your client).

The process for improving the quality of decision-making is well documented, but rarely taught and rarely learned.

Here's a 4-page Business Breakthrough report that delves into the science of decision-making and signposts several resources to build your knowledge on key and valuable decision-making processes. www.paulshrimpling.com/bga-resources and use this access code – **bga-resources2018** – to open the resources from this webpage.

What's the point if there's no action?

Great decisions are clearly valuable to any and every business owner.

The value only really shows up, though, when the business owner follows through.

Why not have a constructive conversation to help your client make a decision AND help your business owner agree specific actions to carry out the decision?

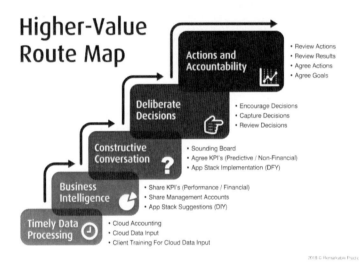

Actions and accountability on those actions can be seen as massively valuable to an isolated and extremely busy business owner.

Here's Andrew Botham talking about the power of actions:

> *"...actions are fundamental enough that they will help the business owner get to where they want to be quicker"*

A business owner reaching his or her goals quicker delivers deep and powerful feelings, as well as crystal-clear demonstration of value too.

Rob Walsh of Clear Vision Accountancy makes a big deal of being clear on who is responsible (accountable) for the different areas of his client's business – marketing, sales, operations, finance, HR, IT and admin.

Clarity on 'who owns what action' is important to Rob and his team.

The ROI of actions

In fact, the accountability on actions plays an important role in Rob's initial (paid for) 'Vision Day' with clients. Rob suggests that the conversation concerning 'who does what' is one of the reasons clients commit to long-term advisory work with him and his team.

> *"...(we) talk about the action points and then we talk about the next stage going forward and when they want the next meeting and when we suggest the next meeting is going to be held"*

And at the next meeting Rob and his team insist on an accountability conversation.

> *"...if the owner of the business is not willing to stand up and be accountable to his own business, how can you expect the team to be accountable for what they are doing? So, he*

needs to lead by example and stand up there and take it on the chin."

Study the full interview with Rob[12] and you'll see how his deliberate focus on decisions and actions wins Rob business. Actions and accountability wins business because of the credibility and reliability connected with being committed to helping the business succeed.

Do what Rob does at the 'next' meeting, and your follow-through and accountability of 'promised' actions has future value the business owners will value and also pay for.

In my own experience of working with accountants in an advisory role, it's usually the meetings with the greatest accountability that are seen as the most valuable.

Not letting clients 'off the hook' has real value and is appreciated, so why not try it out? Why not build your conversation towards actions and accountability?

The depth of feelings your clients experience about you and your firm increases as you step up from Timely Data Processing to Business Intelligence to Constructive Conversations to Deliberate Decisions to Actions and Accountability.

---

[12]   *Get   instant   access   to   Rob's   interview   at www.paulshrimpling.com/bga-resources and use this access code –* **bga-resources2018** *– to open the resources from this webpage or use http://bit.ly/2plWsea*

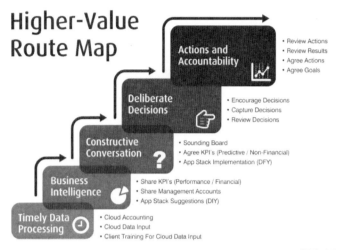

And when you do climb the Higher-Value Route Map, your clients will appreciate you more, much more.

And as a result, you'll be tapping into the four big outcomes you seek for your firm – Client loyalty – Willingness to buy more from you – Willingness to recommend you and your firm – Willingness to pay you more for what you do.

Climbing the 'Higher-Value Route Map' also proves to your clients you genuinely care about their success, you're leading with your heart...

4

Right at the heart of your firm

> *"...I think the true definition of professionalism is caring for our clients."*
>
> *Steve Major, Pricing Power*

This chapter started out being called "A Worthy Mindset".

But the interviews pointed to something more important than mindset (we'll get to powerful mindset insights in a later chapter).

What matters much more than mindset to the most successful Business Growth Accountants?

The interview with Luke Smith of Purpose (Jersey) captures it forcefully:

> *"...basically, it comes down to knowing the theory and giving a shit, and that's it"*

Luke goes on to say:

"Do I really want to spend my life getting involved that deeply with people? – and the answer to that is, 'Yes, I do'."

Rob Walsh of Clear Vision Accountancy Group has built his £1m advisory and accountancy business on the back of one underlying value:

"We care to make a bloody difference."

Wanting to make a difference is a common thread running through all the interviews we conducted. Here's another:

"We change the lives of our clients by helping them grow, we increase their profits, reduce their tax bills and plan for exits"

Aynsley Damery, Tayabali Tomlin

As much as 'mindset' matters, it matters less than 'heartset'.

> *"...you're doing it because you come from a place of help*
>
> *...the number one rule is to be caring, to be interested in them*
>
> *...it's about genuinely being interested in them as a person and their business."*
>
> *Amanda Fisher, CFO & Business Mentor*

The most successful Business Growth Accountants genuinely care for their clients. To these firms, heart is more important than mind, it seems.

Watch out for efficiency thinking

It's easy for accountants to get sucked into thinking efficiently about being a business growth accountant. Watching the clock, keeping a track of minutes or hours rather than feelings and decisions and actions.

If you've ever been rushed out of a restaurant before you and your friends were ready to go, you know that efficiency has a serious client loyalty downside. Like Bernadette Jiwa elegantly points out[13]:

---

[13] *Taken from Bernadette Jiwa's excellent blog* http://thestoryoftelling.com/?s=who+cares *or use* http://bit.ly/2IxCfeh

"In any well-oiled restaurant or company, every individual understands their role in the value chain.

But efficiency is only one element of a great product or experience.

...We know that meeting an expectation is an end to end process, which begins before the customer arrives and finishes as she leaves.

...The things that delight us are born in moments when people who care bring their skills together to create a future they want to see. Care first. Strategise later."

Just like all the business growth accountants interviewed for this book who care first and work on strategy second.

Right at the heart of being a Business Growth Accountant is caring about your clients. Caring about your clients is a worthy activity, and one at which you are well-placed for success.

But where or how does it all start as a Business Growth Accountant?

How do you get going?

What triggers your first step?

What prompts any accountant to pursue a business advisory accountancy life rather than a compliance-only accountancy life?

Something either is prompting you, or has already prompted you, to take your first advisory steps.

The reasons for starting on advisory, as given by the firms interviewed for this book, are many and varied:

- Some accountants want to make a genuine difference to the lives of their clients from the start, as Luke Smith and Steph Hinds did.

- Some accountants are bored and want to do more stimulating and enjoyable work, like Paul O'Byrne and Paul Kennedy.

- Some accountants, like Andrew Botham, simply want to cross-sell more services to existing clients.

- Some, like most firms, want to secure the future of their firm.

- Some want to do less work for higher fees.

- Some simply stumble on the merits of business advisory (business growth) work and then realise this is what they want their life's work to be, like Rob Walsh did

Either you'll be (or have already been) deliberate and organised in getting your first advisory work, as Paul

O'Byrne and Paul Kennedy of O'Byrne & Kennedy were when they made the strategic decision to pursue advisory work...

...or maybe your first business advisory work will happen (or has happened) by accident, or by chance, as it did with Rob Walsh at Clear Vision.

Either way, your first Business Growth client tells you that some business owners have an appetite for help, guidance and support.

Your first advisory client

Every accountancy firm involved in the research for this book and, in fact, every advisory-focused firm (and it applies to your firm too) has to start with a first advisory client.

Your first Business Growth client proves to you that you can and should charge for this service.

Steve Major points to what we could call a match made in heaven:

> *"...accountants bring a set of skills in being able to look at numbers and ask deeper questions of a business. That's a set of skills that's phenomenally valuable when coupled with the entrepreneurial intuition of most small business owners."*

"...I just think that accountants bring an incredible skillset to the table."

Rob Walsh stumbled on his first advisory client and saw a way to win more fees from an existing client. Rob then realised that an advisory approach could be a bona fide service for other business owners and he won more Business Growth work and fees.

And then Rob started to realise that the work he most wanted to do was work that meant he and his team could "care to make a bloody difference".

Rob's mission evolved as he did more and more Business Growth work and eventually Rob's mission became his primary driver for the work he and his firm Clear Vision does.

What is driving you as you start on this Business Growth Accountancy journey?

Is it one of the above bullet-pointed reasons, or is it something different?

Does your reason for starting matter?

The conclusion I've reached is that your initial driver for doing work as a Business Growth Accountant matters not.

However, it pays to beware of being too money-obsessed.

Steve Major is a chartered accountant. He trained with a big firm. He set up his own small advisory firm and now advises accounting firms that are committed to what Steve calls 'business transformation'.

Steve points to the book 'True Professionalism' by David Maister as a source of inspiration for his way of looking at the role of the accountant – and hence his quote to start this chapter.

Here's a quote from Maister himself that underpins the professional values and principles behind successful business advisory, successful business transformation, successful business growth accountancy:

> *"...whenever a professional is trying to sell something, there is only one question on the client's mind: "Why are you trying to sell me something?"*
>
> *There are two possible conclusions the client could come to:*
>
> *First, he or she might believe that the professional is trying to sell something just to get more revenue.*
>
> *Or, second, the client might believe that the professional is trying to sell something because he or she is interested in the client, truly cares, and is sincerely trying to help."*
>
> *David H Maister*

So, when you get going, if your driver is exclusively about the money then you're in danger of losing trust, losing out and losing your way.

If you haven't seen the movie 'Jerry Maguire' it's worth knowing that success finds Jerry (played by Tom Cruise) because he learned to genuinely care. For Jerry Maguire, eventually it **WASN'T** exclusively about...

Show me the money!

Can you be a genuine, trustworthy, credible Business Growth Accountant if it's just about the fees and profits and cash?

The answer to this, according to David Maister, Charles Green and Robert Galford[14], is 'NO, you can't.'

This was also something Steve Major touched on.

> *"...the relationship the advisor has with the small business owner is a very intimate relationship. We might not necessarily be comfortable with that word, but that's the reality. We understand*

---

[14] *The Trusted Advisor by David Maister, Charles Green and Robert Galford. The trust equation the authors suggest makes you think about the practicalities of maintaining and growing trust. You can get a full appreciation of the trust equation from Charles Green's website here http://bit.ly/2pohiuh or for the full url visit http://trustedadvisor.com/why-trust-matters/understanding-trust/understanding-the-trust-equation*

> *their lives so much because we understand*
> *what's going on with their money."*

Steve is pointing to a high-quality and deep relationship.

This depth of relationship trust does not happen when you're doing it exclusively for the cash. We'll cover more on trust shortly but whilst we're talking money...

...will business owners really pay for you to advise them and their business?

Will business owners pay for your advisory help?

Before we get into the research statistics on how many business owners will pay for advice, here's a perspective from one of our Business Growth Accountant interviewees. Steph Hinds of GrowthWise, describes the attitude of her 300+ Australian clients:

> *"We're a business, in Newcastle in Australia,*
> *working predominantly with a bunch of different*
> *small business owners who have one thing in*
> *common, and that's that they're all looking to*
> *improve their business in one way or another."*

All of the GrowthWise clients are 'looking to improve their business in one way or another'.

Peter Taaffe of BWM Chartered Accountants in England provides a Virtual FD service for clients charging from

£3,500 up to £35,000 a year. Here's Peter's thoughts on how 'open' his business owners can be to help and advice:

> *"...clients who know that they're missing a trick, know that there's a gap in their armoury, that they need to run their business better, to take them on to the next level.*
>
> *Or indeed they haven't realised it but in conversation with us, they actually come to realise that this is something they really could benefit from.*
>
> *Typically, it's smaller businesses that are of a size and scale that can't in isolation afford a full-time FD in their own right, but nonetheless, they're big enough to actually need and benefit from the skillsets. That's where we come in, because we fill a gap.*
>
> *Those that don't realise that they could benefit are probably less in number than those who know they need it, in fairness. I think most of the time, we're pushing against that door."*

Pushing against an open door.

UK research backs these anecdotal views up to the hilt. According to a large-scale UK study of 15,502 owners and managers, commissioned by the Department for Business, Innovation and Skills, published in 2016[15].

The research shows the median average amount a business will pay for business advice was £2,000 in 2016.

But it can be much more.

Here's a more comprehensive view from the research on what employers are paying for business advice:

The mean average paid by medium-sized businesses that paid for advice was just under £24,000, compared with just over £9,000 for micros (micro businesses).

However, because of some high sums paid, the median gives a better indication of the amounts that were typically paid by SMEs for advice. Overall, the median was £2,000 (£1,750 for micros, £3,500 for small businesses and £7,000 for mediums).

Your clients, or 22% of them, could be paying you between £1,750 and £7,000 for your advice and face-to-face guidance. But could be paying upwards of £24,000, like the

---

[15] *You can locate the full survey here*
https://www.gov.uk/government/uploads/system/uploads/atta chment_data/file/522364/bis-16-227-sme-employer-report.pdf
It might be easier typing BIS RESEARCH PAPER NUMBER 289 into Google or visit the shortened url http://bit.ly/2FUUeJU

business-owner clients of some of the firms we interviewed for this book.

Here's Hannah from Futrli taking issue with the statistics: accountants sometimes suggest:

> *"...for those accountants that say... advisory only really applies to 20% of my clients...*
>
> *Nonsense, absolutely nonsense!*
>
> *Every single business should run with a plan, every single business wants that security blanket of another educated and trained pair of eyes making sure that they're on the right track, and picking up on things that they haven't necessarily been trained to do... you (accountants) can deliver a hugely valuable service."*

If we stick with the statistics though, one conclusion you could draw from this is that if less than 22% of your existing clients aren't paying you between £1750 and £7000 for business advice and guidance, you're missing out. Simply start having more face-to-face business advisory (business growth) conversations with more clients and you'll uncover a windfall of fees and profits and be on your way to Business Growth Accountancy success.

I emphasize the face-to-face aspect because your clients value the experience you give them. Whilst everything the human race makes gets cheaper[16], as Kevin Kelly succinctly points out in his book 'The Inevitable', there is something more than cost involved:

> *"Just about everything we make, in every industry, is headed in the same economic direction, getting cheaper every day."*

> *"That leaves the big question in an age of plentitude: What is really valuable?"*

Kevin answers his own question:

> *"The only things that are increasing in cost while everything else heads to zero are human experiences."*

And Kevin suggests your source of future income and capital value lies in the experience you give your business-owner clients:

> *"...humans excel at creating and consuming experiences. This is no place for robots. If you want a glimpse of what we humans do when the robots take our current jobs, look at experiences.*

---

[16] *According to a 2002 paper published by the International Monetary Fund "There has been a downward trend in real commodity prices of about 1 percent per year over the last 140 years." – from 'The Inevitable', by Kevin Kelly. Copper prices show this trend and you'll see how a £300 laptop gets faster and more powerful every six months and the new LED TV is half its initial price in six months' time.*

> *That's where we will spend our money (because they won't be free) and that's where we'll make our money."*

The value of a face-to-face experience also shows up in the research by the International Federation of Accountants (IFAC)[17]. The IFAC report delves into the role of small and medium sized accounting practices (SMPs) in providing support for small and medium sized businesses (SMEs). They have reviewed literature published since 2010 on this area and conclude that:

> *"...the preferred form of communication between SMEs and SMPs remains face-to-face"*

Video killed the radio star

But does the client experience have to be exclusively face-to-face? Amanda Fisher thinks not:

> *"I run most of my meetings via Skype or Zoom or, you know, one of those type of platforms so that we can see each other. I send the reports to them in advance of that meeting."*

---

[17] *'THE ROLE OF SMPs IN PROVIDING BUSINESS SUPPORT TO SMEs – New Evidence' – commissioned by IFAC*

In my conversation with Paul Dunn for this book, I asked him whether he'd put the value of a Zoom or Skype call in front and in advance of a face to face meeting?

Paul was very firm in suggesting that a video call delivers greater value than a face-to-face experience. Here's why:

> *"...you start the meeting at a particular time, you end it at a particular time. You will be really, really focused on it. The only thing you can't do is share some coffee. But, then again, you can deliver some coffee complimentarily to the client after they've finished the call anyway."*

> *"You and I could say, why don't we meet tomorrow morning at 10 o'clock or something like that. And we can because it's just over Zoom and away we go. It's very convenient, you don't have to travel and so on. So, it seems to me that there's no doubt that that's the way we're going to go.*

As we unraveled this aspect of your client's experience, we agreed that what's needed to enhance your client's experience is both. Both face-to-face and Zoom or Skype video calls have their place.

> *"I spent six weeks in Canada just recently, you know, I kept the meetings going. We had them on Skype and they knew that I wasn't in Sydney and it worked really, really well."*

> *Amanda Fisher, CFO and Business Mentor*

The value comes from being more regularly connected and maintaining a deeper relationship which will come from more 'visual' contact.

But there's a limit to Skype and Zoom...

Marriage, births and deaths by Skype?

Not long after the interview with Paul Dunn, I was involved in a face-to-face advisory conversation and found myself wondering "should I run this meeting by Zoom?".

We started discussing how the business could and should be freeing the business owner up to spend more time with family. We then dug into how the extra profits and time away from the business could have a profound impact on his marriage and children. I don't believe we would have reached this depth of conversation (and feelings) on a Zoom or Skype call.

And I reached a firm conclusion, Zoom and Skype will limit the depth of conversation, the depth of questions and feelings (and therefore depth of value) experienced. Some conversations will only happen with a *physical* face-to-face meeting.

Which is why, I guess, that Paul Dunn in our conversation concluded:

> *"Any online experience has got to be supplemented by the whole physical experience as well."*

Zoom and Skype might save you time and travel, but some conversations just will not start unless you are physically in the room with your client. Ignore the value of face-to-face conversations and it will be the most emotive and most valuable conversations that will be missed. And lower value will be delivered as a result.

Zoom and Skype are **efficient** visual connections.

Face-to-face meetings are **deeply effective** connections.

A blend and a balance of both will make you an effective Business Growth Accountant.

However I believe Paul Dunn is right to suggest Zoom and Skype communications can transform a client relationship – this transformation will happen when they replace email as the number one default form of communication.

So, what of the time you invest in advisory work? How much time do you need to spend with clients to earn the fees suggested by the Government's BIS research? Or, even better the sort of fees the advisory firms that contributed to this book earn...

Time in meetings

According to the Government's BIS research:

> *22% of those in England and Wales that received (paid for) advice had up to three hours of advice in total, 46% had up to three days and 31% had three days or more.*

The research suggests that good fees can result from a modest investment of your time. This makes a focus on advisory work worthy of your attention.

Almost half of the businesses receiving advice (46%) had up to three days of advice and, if that resulted in a fee of £7,000, then it looks profitable. Of course, your pricing process will determine your ability to win advisory work at healthy fees (for more on pricing check out chapter 11).

Here are four insights from the BIS research that prove there is an appetite for business growth advice:

1) *33% of SME employers had sought external advice or information in the previous 12 months. This proportion increased by size of business (50% of mediums, 40% of small businesses, 31% of micros).*

2) *In England and Wales, 71% of external advice, and 56% of external information, was delivered face-to-face.*

3) *Of those seeking advice and information 65% of SME employers in England and Wales paid for advice. The median average amount paid was £2,000 (the median average micro businesses paid was £1750; small £3500; medium £7000)*

4) *69% of SME employers aimed to grow the sales of their businesses over the next three years. This was particularly likely to be the*

case for medium-sized businesses (89%, compared to 79% of small businesses and 67% of micros).

The last gem shows that it's worth having a conversation with your business owners about their growth plans – most of them are planning to grow it seems. And if 65% (point 3) of the 33% seeking advice (point 1) paying for advice, then 22% of your clients are ready and willing to pay you.

And the larger your client, the more likely they are to pay for guidance and advice to achieve their plans, as suggested by research finding 1.

Hopefully this research reassures you that there is both the opportunity and the appetite for business growth advice in your client base. And one out of three (33%) prospects you see would also value a business growth conversation.

That business owners are willing to pay, as well as the little time you need to invest, makes it profitable to you as well as valuable to clients.

The scale of the opportunity for a Business Growth Accountant looks to be significant.

The report also outlines the 17 most sought-after subjects[18] for advice and information. Here are the top three topics of most sought-after information and advice:

---

[18] *If you want all 17 you'll find the full research paper here - [18] You can locate the full survey here:*
https://www.gov.uk/government/uploads/system/uploads/attac

a. Business growth

b. Improving business efficiency/productivity

c. Financial advice/info for general running of business

These are all strong domains of accountants and a focus for your questions to your business-owner clients.

It's important to note here that of those businesses seeking advice, business growth was sought by 36% of businesses, 18% sought advice on business efficiency and 16% on finances and general business info.

Business growth is the favoured subject, twice as popular than any other subject.

Another section in the research points to the challenges business owners face.

Here's the list of challenges business owners mention, with the most common mentioned first. It's easy to see why accountants could and should be the business owners' go-to person for guidance and advice – six of the eight challenges are close to the work, knowledge and experience of accountants. Only 'a' and 'e' look outside the remit of a

---

hment_data/file/522364/bis-16-227-sme-employer-report.pdf *It might be quicker to find by typing BIS RESEARCH PAPER NUMBER 289 into Google or visit the shortened url* http://bit.ly/2FUUeJU

typical accountant (but not a Business Growth Accountant):

a. Competition in the market

b. Regulations/red tape

c. Taxation, VAT, PAYE, NI, rates

d. Late payment

e. Staff recruitment and skills

f. Workplace pensions

g. Obtaining finance

h. Availability/cost of suitable premises

It's worth noting one telling comment from the IFAC report:

> *"Relationships established between an SMP (small to medium sized practice) and an SME during the provision of traditional compliance services often lead to additional services, especially business advice (Blackburn and Jarvis 2010; Jarvis and Rigby 2012).*
>
> *However, this link does not always materialise (Jarvis and Rigby 2012; Blackburn et al. 2014).*
>
> *One possible reason is that accountants may not fully respond to SMEs' interest in purchasing*

> *additional services because some SMPs do not want to deliver non-traditional services (Jarvis and Rigby 2012)."*

So, some accountants don't want to deliver non-traditional services.

But isn't the risk of irrelevance too dangerous? And why would you want to leave the door open for a competitor too?

Technology progress, increasing expectations of clients, government intervention, and the desire for advice (based on the BIS study) mean change is inevitable.

And the research suggests that being a Business Growth Accountant both secures your future in a chaotic accounting world and builds fees and profits and, possibly, capital value.

In their report, the IFAC seems optimistic for you and your firm:

> *"...the evolution of SMPs (small and medium sized accountancy practices), coupled with the growing demand for business advice, suggest that SMPs currently, and more so going forward, may play the roles of advisor, confidant, analyst, facilitator, and educator to their clients."*

Steph Hinds' experience of working with 300+ clients with an 'advisory first, accountancy second' approach also has encouraging words for you:

"...people come to us because they don't understand how to improve their business, and often that could be something to do with their numbers, so they may not understand necessarily gross margins and profitability and cashflow and finance and things.

But oftentimes they just don't understand the whole, complete picture in one, and that's what we're often getting referred. They might think they have one tiny little problem but as soon as you start that conversation, the ball rolling, they're just dumping all the things that they don't know how to deal with on our plate, and that literally is our job.

We're part psychologist, part mum, part accountant, part mediator."

Steph and her colleagues engage prospective new clients in conversations about the challenges, difficulties, concerns and issues they have in their business. And as the ball starts rolling, the job they have to do for the business owner gets bigger and more valuable to the business owner, and more lucrative for Steph.

And according to the IFAC[19] research into the literature about accountants supporting business owners:

> *"In general, the desired interaction embodies a long-term, personal relationship based on trust and communication."*

This all suggests that trust comes from deeper conversations about more than just last year's accounts and tax.

It also pays to keep in mind that the **value** the client experiences has an awful lot to do with the depth of **trust** they have for you, their accountant.

Value and trust are joined at the hip.

The science of trust

Maister, Green and Galford have given us an equation that signposts how to build a trusted relationship.

Maister et al. suggest that this (next page) equation helps determine your and everyone's level of trust.

---

[19] *THE ROLE OF SMPS IN PROVIDING BUSINESS SUPPORT TO SMES New Evidence – commissioned by IFAC*

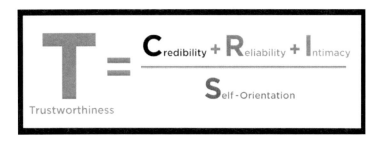

It's worth digging deeper into the equation to see how your role as a Business Growth Accountant fits so well.

When you do things to increase your credibility, reliability and intimacy, trust improves.

And when you do things to reduce your self-orientation, your trust equation also improves.

- **Credibility** arises from your knowledge, insight, experiences and, I would suggest, the quality of the questions you ask. The results you achieve enhance your credibility.

- **Reliability** comes from doing what you said you would, when you said you would. Or from doing it better or faster than expected.

- **Intimacy** means getting close to your clients, empathising with their situation and their feelings. Something as simple as seeing them more often can improve this as well.

- **Self-orientation** is reduced (and trust improved) when your focus, your conversation and your motives are more about your business-owner client and less about you.

Can you see how the last one – self-orientation – is about caring?

If it's entirely about you (show me the money!) then trust will reduce towards zero.

Ask yourself how healthy any intimate relationship is if you do not genuinely care – no matter how credible or reliable you are.

Two elements of trust matter most...

Charles Green's extensive research into this trust equation points to two of the elements being more important than the others.

Increasing intimacy and reducing self-orientation get you the biggest trust wins.

What does this mean in simple, practical terms?

- Go and see you clients more often

- Ask insightful, better questions about them, their situation, their challenges, their results and expectations

- Demonstrate that you recognise, appreciate and understand the way they are feeling and what they are saying

As a result, intimacy goes up and self-orientation goes down. And therefore, your trustworthiness increases also:

> *"...the bottom line, fundamental message that I've pushed virtually every week of every year I've worked is go and see your clients, go and speak to your clients. Where the relationship lies is where the trust lies. No relationship equals no trust and you can't have a relationship based on one meeting a year or two meetings a year. It's hard enough if it was quarterly, but it's feasible quarterly."*

Paul Dunn

As already stated by Luke Smith there's an obvious path to greater trust and therefore greater success as a business advisory accountant:

> *"...basically it comes down to knowing the theory and giving a shit, and that's it"*

Luke Smith

Unpick Luke's statement and you see the trust equation at work in his favour.

- 'Knowing the theory' increases credibility

- 'Giving a shit' shows intimacy and demonstrates a lack of self-orientation

Luke, who generally meets his clients monthly, and sometimes more often has three of the four trust elements working in his favour. It's no wonder his average fee is touching £24,000 across his 26 clients! They trust him implicitly to help them be more successful.

What's neat, though, is that without realising, accountants have a head-start on being 'intimate' with their business-owner clients.

A natural head-start

My experiences of working with accountants over the past 15 years is that most of them are good caring people.

It's easy for accountants to care because they do, naturally. Caring comes easily. Expressing it may not be so obvious, but 15 years, thousands of meetings and hundreds of presentations has proved to me that accountants genuinely care about their business-owner clients.

You are naturally well-placed to be your clients' trusted Business Growth Accountant.

And because you're tied to the numbers of your business client, you also have a head-start on other types of (non-accountant) business advisors. You're already seen as a credible numbers expert.

Shift your conversation onto timely numbers, filtered business intelligence and onto key predictive numbers (see chapter 9) and you start to wonder why a business owner would choose anyone but you and your firm to help them grow.

And what about being reliable?

Because accountants are typically process driven, systematic in their approach and happy to follow checklists, reliability should almost be a given.

Hopefully you can now see that the trust equation clearly works in a way that favours accountants. This should give you good reason to be confident about doing work as a Business Growth Accountant.

A word of warning

It was disappointing to see in the research[20] that accountants are the number one go-to person for business advice **only half the time**.

Other (non-accountant) business advisors get 50% of the requests for help.

Maybe accountants only get half the work because they have yet to ask for the work or demonstrate that they can do advisory work.

The opportunity is significant if you go and grasp it.

Is something holding you or your colleagues back?

---

[20] *You can locate the full survey here* http://bit.ly/2FUUeJU *or visit*
https://www.gov.uk/government/uploads/system/uploads/attachment_data/file/522364/bis-16-227-sme-employer-report.pdf

I suggest you already know that your mindset ultimately determines your actions...

...your mindset determines your success.

5

Your growth mindset essentials

"Is a person's intelligence, character, skill and creativity static, or are these things that can be cultivated?"

Carol S. Dweck

Your answer to this question is critical.

It's critical because of a small but important insight into the science of mindset.

What is the critical insight?

...it's whether we answer YES or NO to Carol Dweck's question above.

> ➤ Say YES and we have a growth mindset

> ➤ Say NO and we have a fixed mindset

This might sound a bit glib, but research into growth mindsets versus fixed mindsets with 160,000 children[21] points to the success that comes from a growth mindset.

What is massively reassuring is that Carol Dweck's life's work into mindset has applied scientific research and has proven that Henry Ford was right all along when he said:

"Whether you believe you can do a thing or not, you are right."

Henry Ford

---

[21] *160,000 10th grade students in the country of Chile showed that holding a growth mindset predicted academic achievement at every socioeconomic level. Another study of 100,00 middle school children showed a similar result. In addition, a study of 113 research papers concluded that mindsets are a significant factor in a person's self-regulation towards goals.*

So, whether you think you can be a successful Business Growth Accountant or you can't, you're absolutely right.

Choose a growth mindset and it's simply a matter of learning.

If you think you or your colleagues CAN'T become a Business Growth Accountant, you have a fixed mindset.

If you think you CAN, you have a growth mindset.

> *"A growth mindset is about believing people can develop their abilities. It's that simple."*
>
> *Carol S. Dweck*

Learning new skills isn't easy, there will be struggle. Dweck points to the importance of the struggle and your response to the struggle:

> *"Learning mindsets come into play right at the point at which we begin to struggle or face a challenge. How we interpret this adversity affects our motivation to remain engaged with the task at hand."*

Believe you can develop the skills to become a Business Growth Accountant and you can handle the struggle! Believe you can't and the struggle will defeat you.

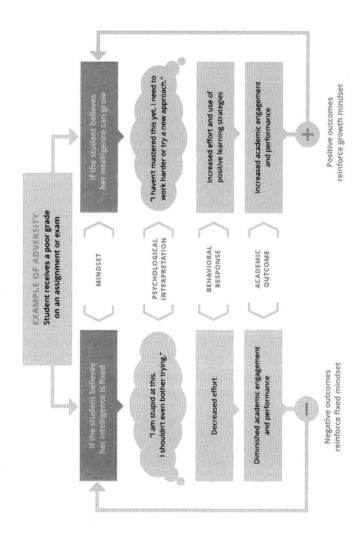

Compare and contrast a growth mindset with a fixed mindset on Carol Dweck's diagram above. It shows how the two mindsets[22] respond to difficulty or challenge.

It's your response to the difficulties and challenges that determine whether you grow. Or whether you stand still whilst others pass you on the road to a brighter Business Growth Accountancy future.

Accountants' contrasting mindsets

When we quizzed Steve Pipe – chartered accountant, author and lifelong commentator on the profession – he pointed to two contrasting mindsets in accountants.

Steve started by describing a perfect example of what Carol Dweck calls the fixed mindset:

> *"...(accountants) take one tiny piece of evidence, one setback, let's say we have a conversation with one prospect or one client that might be vaguely business advisory and it doesn't go perfectly, we extrapolate from that, that it will never work, we'll never be able to do this, they'll*

---

[22]*To delve deeper into the research and science of mindset check out these websites: https://www.mindsetworks.com/ - https://www.ted.com/talks/carol_dweck_the_power_of_believing_that_you_can_improve - https://mindsetonline.com/index.html (also see shortened url http://bit.ly/2FImxiu)*

*never want it. They'll never pay us proper fees
for it, and so on."*

Steve Pipe

Steve then goes onto describe the growth mindset of other accountants. What distinguishes the confident, busy, successful Business Growth Accountant from the less confident accountant?

*"...instead of taking setbacks as evidence that it
will never work and there's nothing they can do
and they might as well give up now, they just
take setbacks as one of those learning points.*

*And they carry on because they're secure in the
belief that this is worth doing, they will end up
finding a way of launching it in the marketplace
and getting paid for it and building their
credibility and so on."*

That's Steve Pipe recognising the growth mindset of other Business Growth Accountants. Carol Dweck's research shows the way and Steve instinctively recognises that the response to the struggle determines the level of success.

Clearly some accountants believe they can and therefore do become successful Business Growth Accountants, while others do not.

Paul Kennedy backs up this view when he talks about his (now sadly deceased) partner Paul O'Byrne and his approach to launching their business growth service:

"Paul would have a go at doing things with no idea how to do them, because he had that philosophy of life. He was never afraid to fail at something. And his idea was that, unless we started failing at consulting, we were never going to get good at it."

"...that's a very unusual mindset in our profession. You know, people want to be totally competent before they do anything. If you take that approach with business advisory work, you'll never get good at it."

Paul Kennedy

Pure growth mindset. Positively dealing with the struggle.

And when you realise that Paul O'Byrne and Paul Kennedy took their 450-client firm to a 50-client firm in little more than a year while still achieving almost the same fees, you can see that a growth mindset works for accountants in the extreme, if they want it to.

If Carol Dweck and her research team is right, all that's required is a change of mindset.

You can manage the struggle if you believe you can. Just like you managed the struggle involved in learning to drive...

45.5 million people can't be wrong

Carol Dweck's research points to the fact that the skill of being a Business Growth Accountant is a skill that can be learned.

Just as anyone can learn a new skill – such as driving a car – you or anyone in your team can learn to become a Business Growth Accountant.

'L' plates will be needed to start with, but a genuine growth mindset approach can set you up for advisory success.

Yes, some accountants will be better than others, but every accountant can learn and build the skills of being a brilliant Business Growth Accountant.

Just as most people learn to drive a car.

The DVLA reported on 30th September 2015 that 45.5 million people held a valid driving licence in the UK.

That's the vast majority of adults who learned something new, a new skill. And every driver has made mistakes and learned from those mistakes and gone on to pass their test.

Is there any reason to suggest the same can't happen if an accountant wants to be a Business Growth Accountant?

45.5 million learners became drivers.

It follows that every accountant can become a successful Business Growth Accountant because the skills can be cultivated:

"Is a person's intelligence, character, skill and creativity static, or are these things that can be cultivated?"

Carol S Dweck

How many accountants in your firm can become Business Growth Accountants?

Answer?

All the ones with a growth mindset. All the ones willing to deal with the struggle, like Aynsley Damery and his team at Tayabali Tomlin...

"...embedded in the culture of the organisation is always striving for continuous improvement, always challenging the status quo and trying to think differently, and we seem to have that culture embedded throughout the organisation"

That's Aynsley describing how he and his team have wired their whole firm with a growth mindset.

Of course, there will be fast learners and slow learners.

Here's one thing that determines whether you're a fast or slow learner (along with your commitment to a growth mindset)...

Your attitude to failure is crucial

It's your attitude to failure that determines your success as a Business Growth Accountant.

Mistakes are inevitable, even necessary.

Mistakes are a source of knowledge, but only to someone who sees a mistake as a learning opportunity.

In fact, the neuroscience of your brain makes mistakes a necessity.

The way your brain works means that if you want to be successful at something new (such as learning to drive) you have to make mistakes, right at the edge of your existing skill level. In short you have to struggle, it's part of the process.

Watch a baby learn to walk and you watch them struggle, you watch them build the skill of walking (by falling over). Building the skill is as much about the laying down of myelin wraps on the nerve fibres in the brain as it is about the muscle development for the act of walking.

The signal speed of a new behaviour down the pathways of your brain has been proven to be two miles per second.

But for a well-practiced skill, the speed jumps to 200 miles per second because the nerve fibres in your brain have been insulated every time you practice (by a substance called myelin). Get 50 myelin wraps by practicing at the edge of your skill level, and you'll be heading towards expert status.

> *"With practice, training, and above all, method, we manage to increase our attention, our memory, our judgement and literally to become more intelligent than we were before."*
>
> *Alfred Binet - creator of the IQ test*

Like Dweck, Binet is answering a timeless and universal question – are your human qualities carved in stone or can they be cultivated?

The inventor of the IQ test argues strongly for the fact that all intelligence qualities **CAN BE IMPROVED**:

> *"A few modern philosopher's assert that an individual's intelligence is a fixed quantity, a quantity which cannot be increased. We must protest and react against this brutal pessimism.... With practice, training, and above all, method, we manage to increase our attention, our memory, our judgment and literally to become more intelligent than we were before."*
>
> *Alfred Binet*

You learn to walk and talk, by making mistakes.

You learn to drive, by making mistakes.

You learn to be a Business Growth Accountant, by making mistakes.

Easier for some than others

I had the great privilege of working with Peter Thomson, a great trainer and advisor to business owners.

One of Peter's famous phrases is:

"People won't consistently do who they aren't"

Basically, he's saying we're hard-wired to behave in particular ways – which according to Carol Dweck sounds like a fixed mindset.

One of my personal challenges with this growth mindset thing is the opposition from the field of psychometric profiling.

Different profiling tools such as DISC profiling from Thomas International, Myers Briggs and many others provide a scientific way of describing our natural behaviour tendencies.

These psychometric profiling tools confirm our natural tendencies and signpost what we're 'hard-wired' to do. Again, promoting a fixed mindset.

But knowing that anyone can learn to drive or that anyone can learn to draw expertly with the right training, means that any skill can be learned and mastered.

So, if there's a desire to change **AND** there's a growth mindset, the existing 'hard-wiring' can be rewired, can't it?

Many actions generate many myelin wraps on the Business Growth Accountant's brain fibres.

With guidance, coaching, mentoring and learning it's possible for every accountant to grow to be a Business Growth Accountant (just as almost every adult learns to drive).

Clearly, those who's psychometric profile lends them better to the skills of being a Business Growth Accountant, will be the better Business Growth Accountants. However the Business Growth skills of asking questions and listening are skills that can be learned and applied. Just like learning to drive can be learned and applied.

But mindset isn't enough

Like the Zen saying suggests:

"...to know and not to do is still not to know."

You can read how-to manuals, attend courses and listen to advice, but unless you get on a bike and have a go you will never really know how to ride a bike.

Yes, you'll fall.

But do you then believe you can't do it, or do you get back on the bike and have another go?

Your growth mindset and ambition to ride will help with this.

Growing into a successful, valuable, impactful business advisor requires you to 'get on the bike' and, yes, fall off a few times.

Go and do. Take action. Start behaving like a Business Growth Accountant:

- Prepare some smart, obvious and enquiring Business Growth questions (see chapter 7)

- Practice listening with your eyes as well as your ears (see chapter 7)

- Share your insights with others in your team and with other business owners

But what if you're wobbling?

What if you're unsure or anxious about the mistakes you'll make along the way?

Firstly, remember it's normal to be uncertain, anxious or even a little scared. It's all part of the struggle.

All you need to do is take the next step...

Stepping stones to success

Learning new things exposes you to error and even a little embarrassment, but your growth mindset helps you recognise this and have another go anyway.

It's as corny as the hills, but your 'mistakes are your stepping stones to future success'.

If you're wondering whether you can or you can't, check out which mindset best reflects your current thinking towards business advisory work. And remember you can choose to change your thinking by simply learning something new and having a go.

And this involves something as simple as asking a relevant and well-crafted question. More on the essential skill of asking questions coming up in chapter 7.

Yes, you'll meet a few challenges and obstacles and will make a few mistakes, but that's OK, it's good for you, good for your brain, good for your skills and good for your future!

> *"When you operate on the edge of your ability, when you are reaching, failing, reaching again, learning velocity goes way up. It goes way up."*
>
> *Daniel Coyle*

133

For more on the power of mistakes, on building myelin and growing signal speed in your brain, check out 'The Talent Code' by Daniel Coyle[23].

Or check out this free 4-page Business Bitesize report for a quick but deep insight into what this is all about – use this access code – **bga-resources2018** – to get the resources from this webpage www.paulshrimpling.com/bga-resources

Lifetime learning

Another common theme arising from the interviews for this book is the pursuit of lifetime learning by all the successful Business Growth Accountants. Books, courses, webinars, events and podcasts are all consumed avidly.

More on this life-long learning attitude in chapter 8.

If you have a learning mindset, your attitude to making mistakes is very different from a 'set in its ways' mindset.

---

[23] *'The Talent Code' by Daniel Coyle is a stunning insight into how one modest tennis club in Russia produces more top-tier tennis players than most countries. And how one tiny Mexican island produces more top-tier baseball players than most US states. And how a lowly Yorkshire football team beat two international sides. It's not talent, it's skill development (growth mindset) and a healthy attitude to failure.*

And yet everyone can learn a new skill if they choose to. Just as everyone (45.5 million) can learn to drive a car.

What if you could reduce the chances of mistakes by learning about what successful Business Growth firms do and how they do it?

Are you ready to don a set of Business Growth 'L' plates?

Then start learning and building your skill at asking great questions...

> *"...the important discovery that the best path to helping people learn is not to tell them anything but to ask the right questions and let them figure it out."*
>
> *Edgar H Schein*[24]

Actually, the evidence we've captured from our interviews suggests that it's not asking great questions but asking simple questions that is most effective.

There's a drastic alternative

Meet too much resistance to change and what do you do?

---

[24] *From 'Humble Consulting: How to Provide Real Help Faster' by Edgar H Schein*

Meet a 'fixed-in-reinforced-concrete' mindset and what do you do?

When we interviewed Nick Williams (Head Of Business Development at Intuit QuickBooks) he talked about a couple of the more technology-advanced and advisory-advanced top 100 firms – Wilkins Kennedy and Kingston Smith.

Here's what Nick is hearing:

> *"They're saying, truly, what talent do we need?*
>
> *Well actually, to try to be more business advisory, let's get more consultancy led and advisory-like people in, with a level of much deeper client interaction, almost sales level interaction with the customers.*
>
> *...mindset of, like, business first, thinking about improvement. It's being very customer-led, very customer-supportive, that's what we're seeing."*

What these firms are doing is investing in their existing accountants, and at the same time looking at recruiting people better suited to advisory work. These firms are...

> *"...bringing in graduates from business or people who have been a business consultant or someone with a level of consultancy experience"*
>
> *Nick Williams, Intuit*

Here's Hannah Dawson from Futrli commenting on how a Business Growth Accountancy approach can help you recruit the right people:

> *"...to facilitate the hiring plans... a lot of accounting firms are going to have to offer something a little bit different.*
>
> *(Accountants) are going to make a choice... 'Am I going to be doing tax returns every day, or can I go out and visit clients and actually effect a change on their business?'"*

This is a common conversation I'm experiencing with many of the accounting firms I advise, consult and meet with. Peter Taaffe of BWM suggests recruiting non-accountants:

> *"If you can source people who have got wider experience, who have actually been in business themselves, to join the team to compliment what you're doing, that helps enormously because it is a different mindset, it is a different place to go, because the clients issues as often as not, can't be solved by staring at accounts."*

Here's Aynsley Damery from award-winning firm Tayabali Tomlin sharing his recruitment preferences:

> *"...we're not looking for accountants who just want to sit behind a screen and play with numbers. That's important and there is a role for that but we're looking really for accountants*

who've got their commercial awareness, who've got their technical ability as well.

...they've got a commercial awareness, they've got great communication skills and they can understand and talk to clients."

Every firm, your firm, needs to be seen to be adopting technology and providing greater value by having more valuable conversations. This means more of your people asking more questions and having more meaningful and valuable conversations with business owners.

But before we get deep into the art and science of questions, what about the global mindset of your firm, otherwise known as your firm's market positioning?

6

Time to put accountancy 2nd?

When asked what distinguishes the top advisory firms from the rest of the firms he's been exposed to, Steve Major points to mindset as well.

But Steve approaches mindset from a different viewpoint, a market positioning view point.

Steve acknowledges the relevance of a 'value-added services' mindset, but he then suggests this 'value-added' mindset is unhelpful. Here's why...

Steve sees this 'value-added' mindset as wrong, back-to-front, in fact:

> *"...the firms that are that top 5% or 10%, the firms that really crack the code on business advisory, make it business advisory first."*

> *Steve Major*

Steve is suggesting that 'value added services' is the wrong mindset because the best firms are not adding Business Growth services to accountancy.

The best firms start with Business Growth and then add accountancy!

The best firms put accountancy in 2nd place.

Here's Steph Hinds of GrowthWise making it clear how her firm works with business owners:

> *"People cannot be a GrowthWise client unless they have advisory. We just don't give them a choice."*

Steve Major confirms this:

> *"...how can we help that small business grow, change, transform, whatever that small business owner wants to achieve out of that business?*

> *That (growth) needs to be the primary focus, and then yes, we are still accountants, so we still do all the compliance and tax obligations etc."*

Steve thinks that the 'value added' mindset can trip you up.

Thinking 'value-add' prevents your firm being the best it can be at business advisory.

He also points to the firm's strategy:

> *"...it's having the mindset first and foremost. That everything revolves around the business transformation service that we can put together, rather than going where accountants equals compliance services, and then we try to sell them some added-on services.*
>
> *I think it's flipping that equation and making it business advisory first."*

> *Steve Major*

This putting of advisory first and foremost stood out with most of the firms we interviewed. And when compliance still played a strong role in the firm, the emphasis of the firm's focus, strategy, marketing and culture put advisory to the fore. **These firms do not put accountancy first but a strong second**.

This approach is fundamental to the Business Growth Accountancy fees earned by Andrew Botham, Rob Walsh, Greg Smargiassi, Luke Smith, Steph Hinds, Aynsley

Damery, Paul Kennedy, James Solomons and all the Business Growth Accountants we interviewed.

Advisory first, accountancy a strong second works for these firms. The average fees and the growth and stability of these firms suggests a profound payoff. It also de-risks your firm too:

> *"If advisory is at the heart, then the connection that they have to their client base is far greater. There's a lot less risk as well from their client base"*
>
> *Hannah Dawson, founder of Futrli*

What Hannah is saying is that when you're better connected to your clients (and your clients' numbers) they are less likely to entertain your firm's competition.

Position your firm

Position your firm as a Business Growth Advisory firm first, with accountancy second. Build your firm's processes to deliver Business Growth Accountancy.

Think about the *processes* of being a Business Growth Accountant, not just the end result of happy and successful clients (and healthy fees and profits).

Of course you must use the technology to free up your people's time but remember this is not a technology issue. Timely data processing and reporting is made possible by cloud accounting and gives you and your clients timely accounts data. However, it pays to heed the words of Futrli (software company) founder Hannah Dawson:

> *"...software is not a silver bullet, it's not a silver bullet at all. You can't ever buy a piece of software and suddenly it's going to change your life. There has to be some PROCESS CHANGE or strategy change alongside it, irrespective of what it is."*

Being process-focused helps ensure your success. I know this sounds like I'm stating the obvious, but here's what Jeremy Dean has to say about process in his book 'Making Habits, Breaking Habits'. He's referencing a psychology study into success[25]:

> *"...participants who expected success, rather than fantasising about it, were more likely to take action."*

> *"Participants who visualised themselves reading and gaining the required skills and knowledge spent longer studying and got better grades in the exam than those who only visualised their goal."*

> *"As opposed to fantasising, a more effective way of visualising the future is to think about the*

---

[25] *G Oettingen and D Mayer. 'The motivating function of thinking about the future.: Expectations vs Fantasies.' Journal of Personality and Social Psychology 83, no.5 (2002)*

> *processes that are involved in reaching a goal,*
> *rather than just the end state of achieving it."*

> *Jeremy Dean, 'Making Habits, Breaking Habits'*

See yourself learning and practicing the skills of Business Growth Accountancy (sharing business intelligence, asking great questions and quality listening) and you're more likely to end up learning these skills.

It pays to be ambitious

Setting modest goals can undermine your thinking, your actions and your performance.

> *"Everybody talks about the profession being*
> *disrupted.*

> *But what do we do about that?*

> *Well, I think there's two things that we need to*
> *do. And these aren't 'either-or' choices, these are*
> *choices that are no choices.*

> *The first choice, I think is to play a bigger game.*
> *Just to play a bigger game."*

This is Paul Dunn suggesting a 'stretch' goal for you and your firm, a stretch goal worthy of notice.

When planning your firm's next year, you could do what most firms do and ask: 'how do we get a 10% increase?'

"...instead of asking the 10% question, you should ask the 10 times question. Now when you ask the 10 times question, you may not get to the 10 times answer. But it is certain that you'll get to a better answer than the 10%."

Paul is suggesting you play a serious game of working out how you achieve a 10x achievement for your next year. Such a serious 10x game will result in you and your team generating ideas, insights, ideas and plans that will bring you a better than 10% result.

There's some strong science behind this approach. A summary of more than 1,000 studies into business goals and other goals suggests[26]:

"There is strong evidence that the increases in job performance produced by goal-setting have important economic and practical value."

The research, along with practical experiences at Jack Welch's GE, suggest that **discomfort** is the required emotion to go with your business goals.

Jack Welch was CEO at GE for 20 years. And, like Paul Dunn suggests, Jack pushed for **stretch** goals, not attainable goals. In his 20 years as GE boss he increased the company's market value from $12 billion to $280 billion! It would seem stretch goals are worth it.

---

[26] *'New Developments In Goal Setting and Task Performance' by Edwin A Locke and Gary P Latham*

The Locke and Latham book references an article in The Economist (2011) about GE's stretch goals:

> *"…if the right environment was created for the group, setting stretch goals and working toward what might seem to be impossible results often became reality."*

Stretch goals don't always work

Stretch goals aren't a panacea, as suggested in the research feeding a valuable Harvard Business Review article[27]:

> *"Organisations that would most benefit from them [stretch goals] seldom employ them, and organisations for which stretch goals are probably not a good strategy often turn to them in a desperate attempt to generate breakthroughs."*

The article is definitely worth your attention as it provides some valuable insights into when stretch goals work and when they don't.

The article also suggests alternative goal-setting strategies in different situations – see next page.

---

[27] *https://hbr.org/2017/01/the-stretch-goal-paradox* *try this shortened url see* *http://bit.ly/2GGEPhh*

Are Stretch Goals Right for You?

How would you describe your organization's recent performance?

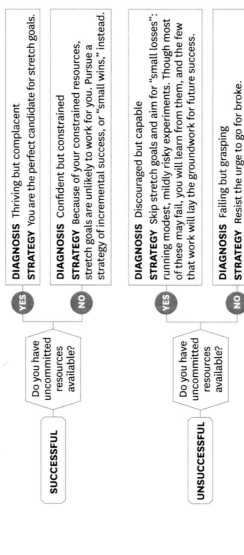

SUCCESSFUL

Do you have uncommitted resources available?

YES

DIAGNOSIS Thriving but complacent

STRATEGY You are the perfect candidate for stretch goals.

NO

DIAGNOSIS Confident but constrained

STRATEGY Because of your constrained resources, stretch goals are unlikely to work for you. Pursue a strategy of incremental success, or "small wins," instead.

UNSUCCESSFUL

Do you have uncommitted resources available?

YES

DIAGNOSIS Discouraged but capable

STRATEGY Skip stretch goals and aim for "small losses": running modest, mildly risky experiments. Though most of these may fail, you will learn from them, and the few that work will lay the groundwork for future success.

NO

DIAGNOSIS Failing but grasping

STRATEGY Resist the urge to go for broke. Pursue "small wins" until you dig yourself out.

FROM "THE STRETCH GOAL PARADOX," BY SIM B. SITKIN, C. CHET MILLER, AND KELLY E. SEE, JANUARY–FEBRUARY 2017 © HBR.ORG

Yes, there's real merit in stretch goals – a conversation worth having within your firm and a conversation worth having with your clients too, don't you think?

If you want an easy-to-read and easy-to-share 4-page report to stimulate conversation around goal setting you can get this Business Bitesize report on 'Stretch Goals' here – www.paulshrimpling.com/bga-resources - use this access code – **bga-resources2018** – to open this webpage.

In our interview, Paul Dunn goes on to suggest a view wider than that of a simple revenue or profit goal:

> *"I like what Seth Godin[28] said not long ago. Seth said, the challenge is not to be successful, the challenge is to matter.*
>
> *...the challenge is how do you move from being dispensable to indispensable?"*

Make your firm indispensable in the minds and hearts of your clients and a 10x result may just be possible for your firm.

---

[28] *Seth Godin is a multi-best-selling author, titles include 'Purple Cow' and 'Tribes' and 'Small Is The New Big'*

Paul is insisting you play a bigger (10x) game AND matter to your client to make your firm indispensable.

> *"So how do we do things that make us matter more? And the answer to that is very, very simple.*
>
> *There are a whole series of behaviours that you will be doing that will be clearly saying to the client, these guys matter.*
>
> *They absolutely matter to us because they are an essential part of our growth. They are an essential part of the way we do business."*

Paul suggests that you and your firm are directly and wholeheartedly connected to the growth of your client's business, but only when you master a 'series of behaviours'.

What Paul means here is questioning behaviours, listening behaviours and other advisory behaviours (including using the technology at your disposal to help share relevant business intelligence).

Business growth is important to clients

Paul talks about being involved in '*the way they do business*' to make you and your firm indispensable.

I believe what Paul is talking about is:

- Help clients with the KPIs that matter

- Help clients build robust systems and processes that provide their KPIs and

- Engage in conversation about the mission-critical KPIs

If you're doing these things I reckon you'll look and feel indispensable to your clients.

You're still the numbers expert. You're talking accountancy however...

...you're talking business growth 1st, accountancy a strong second.

Business Growth 1st because business growth really matters to business owners.

Remember the statistics from the UK government research[29] from over 15,000 businesses?

Of the 17 most sought-after subjects for advice and information, number one was business growth. And business growth advice was sought twice as often as any other form of advice.

Make your firm indispensable and talk business growth. Accountancy plays a role, but it's secondary to your clients.

So, if you're ready to make Business Growth Accountancy 1st in your firm, where do you start?

Here's how you make your firm truly valuable...

---

[29] *You can locate the full survey with all 17 subjects listed here:* https://www.gov.uk/government/uploads/system/uploads/attachment_data/file/522364/bis-16-227-sme-employer-report.pdf *It might be quicker to find by typing BIS RESEARCH PAPER NUMBER 289 into Google or see the shortened url* http://bit.ly/2FUUeJU

7

Make your firm truly valuable...

"The missing ingredients in most conversations are curiosity and willingness to ask questions to which we do not already know the answer."

Edgar Schein from 'Humble Enquiry'

Starting from scratch as a Business Growth Accountant

"How do you start from scratch as a Business Growth Accountant when you've been a compliance-only accountant all your life?"

When James Solomons, Head of Accounting at Xero Australia, started his accounting and advisory business in 2015 he had no clients.

James didn't have case studies or testimonials to prove he could be a trusted business advisor.

He simply focused on building relationships:

"...we've had to rely upon just building a great relationship with that client to trust us and then obviously that doesn't happen straight away."

James suggests here that building a relationship takes time (and effort).

And when we spoke, James made it very clear that relationship building starts with good questions.

The quality of the questions you ask are a visceral and vital aspect of the work you do as a Business Growth Accountant.

"The services that we offer are fairly standard across (accounting firms) but when we ask a question and find out what is troubling (business

> *owners), keeping them up at night, what their growth pains are, we then are able to tailor our response to end the problem they're having"*
>
> *– James Solomons, Head of Accounting at Xero Australia and Co-Founder of Aptus Accounting and Advisory*

In our interview, James makes the point that the value of the discussion with clients and prospects is not around what you do, but around the questions you ask.

He shares an example:

> *"The way that we would apply a budget and forecast to a start-up business might be very different to a business that's just lost a major contract, but we're still going to be doing a budget and forecast to understand the way it is."*
>
> *"But the way that we deliver the solution piece when we're pitching to them and putting a price on it, is key to solving their problems."*

James is saying the solution comes after he understands their issues, challenges and concerns. Understanding the issues comes from asking great questions. The value lies in the questions first, the answers second and the solution third.

Before we hear how James starts client meetings with a simple and obvious question...

...here's an elephant-in-the-room that needs dealing with...

Ambiguity feels so uncomfortable

Why would an accountant who is used to the concrete certainty of a set of accounts embrace the ambiguous uncertainty of asking clients about the future of their business?

This can be enough to put off some accountants from starting business growth conversations.

But why deprive your client of this valuable support?

Here's Kevin Kelly[30] from his book 'The Inevitable' talking about ambiguity and the most valuable and productive facets of our lives:

> *"...the most precious aspects, the most dynamic, most valuable, and most productive facets of our lives and new technology will lie in the frontiers, on the edges where uncertainty, chaos, fluidity, and questions dwell."*

Kelly is suggesting that in a massively changing technological world the questions you ask are massively valuable in their own right.

So, where does this place the question makers like you?

> *"Question makers will be seen, properly, as the engines that generate the new fields, new*

---

[30] *'The Inevitable – Understanding The 12 Technological Forces That Will Shape Our Future' by Kevin Kelly*

> *industries, new brands, new possibilities, new continents that our species can explore.*
>
> *Questioning is simply more powerful than answering."*
>
> *Kevin Kelly*

Paul Dunn shared the following gem about the ambiguity and uncertainty you'll face in client meetings where you're asking business success questions:

> *"...when you're thinking about does the client need advice and should you be giving it to them and all that kind of stuff...*
>
> *...you've got to remember; the golfer can never see his swing. And I thought, oh, that's a lovely way of saying it.*
>
> *And sometimes what we need to understand is that we're not necessarily looking for an answer. What we're looking for is a different way of looking at that issue. In other words, we're looking for a different perception."*

This connects with the idea that Andy Murray wasn't winning major championships until Ivan Lendl showed up. Lendl could see Murray's swing. Lendl almost certainly asked Andy questions about what he was doing and what he was feeling and then got into a discussion about what to change.

In business 'the swing' is the KPIs being measured, the decisions being made, and the actions being taken.

You, the numbers expert, can provide the outsiders view which can result in the equivalent of an Olympic gold medal or a Wimbledon or US Open Trophy.

Try asking questions about KPIs and get your people to try it too. Then review how well your clients respond to you and your colleagues.

Start a Business Growth conversation

When asked about the skills accountants need to be a valuable advisor Hannah from Futrli suggests:

> *"..the first basic is that they're not scared to have a conversation..."*

> *"...and from that, as long as there's that confidence to be able to go, I should have a conversation with my client, I'm not scared, I want to find out about their business... You know, tell me. Talk to me. That's the starting point."*

This then begs the question:

> *"How do you start a successful Business Growth conversation?"*

Here's the question James Solomons uses to start an advisory conversation:

> *"What problems are you having with your business?"*

James acknowledges that this sounds a bit cliché, but it gets a meaningful conversation going. This simple, obvious but meaningful question gets the advisory conversation going.

If you wish, you make the question less confrontational when you simply change the word 'problems' to 'challenges' or 'issues' or 'concerns'.

But what if you prefer to start with a positive tone?

You could start with:

> *"When you think about your business, what are you most proud of in the last 12 months?"*

Having listened and noted the answer, you can then frame James' problem question like this:

> *"...and on the flip side, what problems are you having with your business?"*

> *or*

> *"...now tell me, what issues are you experiencing in your business?"*

So, why not, in your next accounts finalisation meeting, give James' simple opening question a try?

Peter Taaffe runs a successful 60-person practice in Liverpool, with focus on providing a Virtual FD service to clients.

Peter also points to asking the simple and obvious questions:

> *"It's asking the questions and just challenging their thinking all the time, without being a right pain in the arse..."*

> *"...make them think about what they've been doing for the last three years, whether or not there is or isn't a better way."*

Peter also recommends using a caveat to help position your level of expertise and make it easier to ask the simple or stupid questions.

Here's Peter's caveat:

> *"I'm going to ask a really stupid question, but..."*

> *"...The client knows that you are not an expert in construction techniques, and I can't decorate a living room - as my wife will tell you."*

If you're nervous about asking any question that might seem dumb or too simplistic, use Peter's caveat to prepare your client for your dumb question.

> *"...you may feel like an idiot for asking them, but actually, you've got 30 years' worth of experience going into what might seem like an*

> *idiotic question to you, but actually for the client, it might well not be."*

> *"...stupid questions tend to get to the heart of the matter. They tend to be very incisive."*

So, having got your Business Growth conversation going with a simple or even a stupid question, what next?

Work out what questions to ask and when

Sticking with James for a while longer, it's worth noting from an earlier quote that the aim of James' questions is two-fold:

1. Find out what is troubling the business owner

2. Find out about their growth plans and pains

James is using this simple two-part framework to frame his questions and create a meaningful conversation.

When we quizzed Aynsley Damery about conversations with clients he was quick to reel off a series of questions he often asks clients and prospects:

> *"...what are you trying to achieve, where are you going, what do you want this business to do for you? What do you want in five years time? What does the business need to do to deliver that?*

And where are you now versus where you want to be?

...what are the issues for you? What your concerns are, why you're not happy, what you think you're missing?"

Can you see how the questions are simple and relatively easy to ask? And can you see that the power of the conversations that follow are profoundly valuable?

It's worth noting that Aynsley starts the questions even before he meets a new prospect:

"...when somebody comes to us asking to meet, we schedule a phone call and that's generally done with me. So, I will be on the first phone call trying to delve into the issues and concerns."

Before we delve deeper into helpful questioning frameworks, here's a word about compliance.

Beyond compliance

What distinguishes successful Business Growth Accountants from a typical (and successful) compliance accountancy firm?

Business Growth Accountants move from asking compliance-focused questions to ones about the performance of their business, as it happens.

Growth-focused accountants step beyond compliance-based conversations...

Later you'll hear about how Greg Smargiassi uses traditional compliance numbers to stimulate a business improvement conversation.

Yes, you can start with a compliance conversation or you can dive straight into a business growth conversation.

What's clear is that the questions you ask will go way beyond compliance numbers if you're going to be a successful Business Growth Accountant.

Let's now get back to the use of a question framework.

Start collecting question frameworks

This idea of frameworks stood out in my chat with Luke Smith of Purpose in Jersey.

Luke is business advisory first, using accountancy in a support role with his clients. And at the time of the interview he was charging an average fee of £24,500 across his 26 clients.

Luke told me he is always looking for frameworks he can use in his own business as well as frameworks he can use in client advisory meetings too.

> *"It's something that definitely helps me in the advisory meetings I regularly hold with accounting firms – it means I don't have to look far to find a relevant question. Frameworks*

provide a go-to source of great questions and guidance."

Luke Smith

Paul Kennedy from O'Byrne & Kennedy in England also holds firm views about the value of frameworks:

"A mental map of what works in business and what doesn't work in business is what I think you need, and then from there you pull out the questions that compare that successful model with the model that is in front of you, coming out of the lips of the person that you're speaking to."

Paul Kennedy

Steve Major, an advisor to accountants in Australia who specialises in pricing business advisory services, also uses a powerful and memorable framework that builds on James' earlier two-part framework.

Steve suggests three subjects which your questions should cover – here are Steve's three with a handful of example questions:

1. The Pain

What's holding the business back?

What's driving the business owner nuts?

What's creating the stress and worry?

How long has the challenge been holding the business back?

2. The Job

What tasks need attention?

What systems and processes need attention?

What feedback from clients are you getting about the way you deliver what they want?

Who does what, and when, and how well?

3. The Afters

What does success look like?

How should the business perform when it's working to your complete satisfaction?

How would you define success in the next 12 months?

Who would be the first person you'd tell about your success when you get there?

For number 3, Steve talks about Outcomes not Afters. But I like easy-to-remember frameworks, so I changed it to

'Afters' (borrowing from Andy Bounds' book, 'The Jelly Effect[31]').

Using 'Afters' for number 3 means we can use the acronym PJAs (as in pyjamas!). Question PJAs – a great and memorable framework: P-Pain; J-Job; A-Afters.

What's elegant about Steve's 3-part framework is that it is simple and obvious as well.

It wouldn't take you long to take the four questions already listed in each section above, and add another 20 or more, giving you a question 'ready-reckoner' you can use like Martini – any time, any place, anywhere!

Remember the Zen saying?

"...to know and not to do is still not to know."

Give it a go and come up with 60 to 100 PJA questions you can use any time, any place, anywhere! Start by adding just one additional question to each of the PJA sections above.

---

[31] *The Jelly Effect by Andy Bounds. Andy is another master-craftsman when it comes to questions. And questions about 'afters' make so much sense and fit neatly into the SPIN model too. N for needs/payoff are simply 'afters' questions – more on SPIN questions coming up.*

"In what order do you ask the questions?"

> *"...just ask the big questions, and then you get more and more granular once you start to understand the landscape. But to start off with, it's "what are you trying to...?"*
>
> *"Begin with the end in mind" to start with, and then you start to hone in on the detail."*

Paul Kennedy

Paul Kennedy is quoting one of the business classics, Stephen Covey's 7 Habits[32]:

> *"Seek first to understand then be understood"*

Stephen R Covey

Which is another way of saying, ask great questions.

Paul's suggestion to ask questions about the big picture first and then to dig into the detail is a good one.

But how do you work out what specific questions to ask?

---

[32] *The 7 Habits Of Highly Effective People by Stephen Covey. Seek first to understand is habit 5*

The ultimate question framework

This is the one framework you already know naturally and intuitively.

You use it all the time without thinking.

But it pays to think about it.

It's as simple as it gets and simplicity is worth pursuing, as Paul Kennedy points out:

> *"...you've got to keep it simple ...you've got to ask the obvious questions ...I think that's something that we learnt in the early days, is that we used to sort of avoid the obvious ones, we used to try and come up with clever stuff."*

> *"...it's simple stuff, you know. In five years' time, where do you see yourself, what would you like to have achieved? What's stopping you getting there?"*

> *Paul Kennedy*

Paul is urging the use of the simple and obvious question.

Not the smart, clever or complex question.

Don't underestimate the power of a simple and obvious question – like the ones Paul mentions above.

Now what's the simple question framework you already know and love that we mentioned earlier?

Every searching question you'll ever ask will start with one of 6 words:

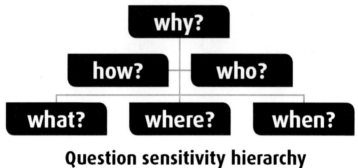

Question sensitivity hierarchy

We'll tackle the hierarchy of the six questions in a moment.

Firstly, can you see how these questions get your business owner client or prospect talking and you listening?

They're called **open questions**. They get you information. They get your client sharing their thoughts, their issues, their frustrations, their wants, their goals, their dreams.

The answers you get from using these six words help you deliver value, without your needing to share anything to do with suggested solutions, plans or actions.

As James Solomons mentioned earlier:

> *"What problems are you having with your business?"*

> *"What would you like to have achieved?"*

"Where do you see yourself?"

And if you needed more inspiration and insight into what questions to ask, Bernadette Jiwa (in one of her wonderful blogs[33]) rightly suggests there are three categories of questions:

1. Questions that can't be answered yet

2. Questions that aren't worth asking

3. Questions not yet considered

It's the third set of questions that challenges, inspires, educates or simply stimulates a meaningful conversation with your client.

It pays to prepare and plan these in advance, not dream them up on the hoof when in the cut-and-thrust of a client meeting. Leave all your questions to chance and you'll likely end up asking questions from Jiwa's groups 1 and 2 and get absolutely nowhere with your client.

Simple stuff.

Listening is simple too but so often the skill of listening is ignored or at the very least taken for granted.

---

[33] http://thestoryoftelling.com/questions-worth-asking/   *for the shortened url see* http://bit.ly/2HKKq5A

Rarely is listening a skill that's taught or developed in accountancy firms. And yet it's a skill that's jugular to your success as a Business Growth Accountant...

Grow big listening ears

"...listening to what the client's problems are may have nothing to do with finance or accountancy, but just listen to them"

Peter Taaffe of BWM Chartered Accountants is advocating learning from listening.

Ask a great question and actively listen to the answer.

Sounds basic.

But so many people aren't genuinely listening.

I bet you can recognise times when you've experienced these different levels of listening from people you care about – and I bet it upset you in some way:

1. **Ignoring** – paying no attention to what's being said

2. **Pretending** – nodding and saying the odd 'yes' or 'mmm' or 'ah hah' but not hearing a thing

3. **Waiting to speak** – listening for the gaps in what's being said so they can speak

These three levels of listening show different levels of ignorance and are very far removed from being a trusted advisor.

Respectful listening requires you to hear the words and the feelings being expressed.

4. **Hearing the words** – Hearing the words that are spoken shows respect but only to a level.

   You can build the skill of listening at this level by practising repeating what people say (in your head – don't do it in a client meeting they'll think you've lost the plot!). I used the radio to help me build this skill before using it with clients. You'll find your recall of what was said improves with this approach.

5. **Hearing and seeing the feelings** – When you see and hear the tone of what's being said it can radically change the meaning of the words.

Try saying the following in a low energy frustrated way:

"I'm really excited about the future of my business."

Or say this in an angry tone and angry face:

"I'm really impressed with the way this meeting has gone."

Acknowledging what's been said and what feelings are being expressed is another skill worth developing.

Repeat, rephrase, reflect

First you listen and hear the words and the feelings.

Second, you REPEAT back to your client what's just been said.

Third, wait and see what's said next.

This 3-stage process demonstrates that you're listening at a deep and respectful level.

Make it even stronger by REPHRASING what's just been said rather than REPEATING what's just been said.

And you go deeper again when you acknowledge the feelings being expressed as well as repeating or rephrasing what's been said.

To help you reflect feelings and rephrase what's being said, use phrases to start your questions like these:

> **"It sounds like** you're upset at the way your business has been performing over the last 6 months"

> **"It looks like** you'd like to relieve some of the stress you're experiencing from all the people changes you're experiencing'

Simple questions.

Respectful listening.

Then repeat, rephrase and reflect the feelings you see and the words you hear.

How would you feel if you were treated to this depth of listening? You'd feel respected and cared for.

Remember Ron Baker's phrase:

> *"Value is not a number, it's a feeling"*

The value you and your firm deliver is wrapped up in the feelings your clients experience.

Great questions and great listening deliver massive value.

The value of a sounding board

Many of the people interviewed for this book suggested great value in being a sounding board for clients.

Amanda Fisher talks about the willingness of clients to pay for a sounding board:

> *"I continue to provide the reports and it's more now around extra advice and a sounding board for her for the decisions she's making.*
>
> *So, for example, a couple of things that have come up over the last few months have been her employee resigned. So, we then (discussed) the process of identifying whether we replaced with another senior person or whether we replaced with a different mix of staff."*

Being a great sounding board requires the skills of questioning, listening and then demonstrating that you've heard your client's words and feelings.

Please do not underestimate the power of a great question.

And never switch off your big listening ears, especially at the end of a meeting:

> *"...listen to what the client is saying once a formal meeting has finished, because they may tell you things that they haven't intended to discuss that actually, lead you onto different areas so the conversation widens out and every which way, you're then providing value."*

Peter Taaffe again pointing to the importance of listening. And often the client just needs a little prompting to voice their own thoughts to reach a conclusion or decision:

"Most times, the client actually knows the answer, it's just they don't know they know the answer"

As mentioned already, there's ambiguity in conversation since you don't know the answer to your question. And one question inevitably leads to more questions – ones you haven't prepared.

But you should...

Never ever run out of questions

Questions using the 'Paint by Numbers' process I'm about to recommend will certainly help.

But what's key here is you learning the skill of crafting good questions, not me or anyone else gifting you with the best questions you could ever ask! This would be almost impossible because of the scale of variables around your different clients and the various issues they will be experiencing.

What matters is your ***question preparation***.

Your questioning skills must improve if you're going to be a profitable, valuable and trustworthy business advisor.

The chances of you crafting great business growth questions in a client meeting whilst thinking on your feet, not sure what you're doing or unsure where the conversation is going, is a big ask. You'll stutter, stall and run the risk of falling on your backside unnecessarily.

Preparation and practice is the key to questioning success.

Start with preparation.

Prepare good questions in the comfort of your firm's meeting room, or at home. It's a great exercise to do in small teams together, and even better if you can set up competing teams to see who comes up with the best and largest number of questions.

Here's the exercise, and you can do it now if you wish – it will only take a few minutes.

1. Take your six questions – what, where, when, who, how and why

2. Take your PJA framework – Problem, Job, Afters

Step 3 requires some action now:

3. Multiply the two – using the 4 example questions for each of PJA given earlier to help get you started:

    a. Write down six more open questions around 'Problems' using the six question words

    b. Write down six more open questions around 'Job' using the six question words

    c. Write down six more open questions around 'Afters' using the six question words

6 x 3 = 18 questions.

If you want to run a team training session on this exercise, you can extend the learning by working on, for each PJA section, 4 x WHAT questions, then 4 x WHERE questions, then 4 x WHEN, WHO, HOW and WHY questions.

Now you have 6 x 3 x 4 = 72 questions.

And we have yet to decide what specifically to ask the questions about!

Problems could be sales, marketing, people, recruiting, production, customer complaints, customer care, technology or distribution.

Now you have 6 x 3 x 4 x 9 = 648 questions.

Start small, though. Keep it simple.

Go for 6 x 3 = 18 questions to start.

Now that you have a large collection of questions you can start to sift the good questions from the bad questions and the ugly questions. But please remember...

> *"...none of it is rocket science. Just really, really ask... And keep asking more questions about, you know, what does it take to do that? Or what fundamentally needs to change for that to happen? Why do you think doing it the way you're doing it now means you're going to get there?"*
>
> *Paul Kennedy*

The question sensitivity hierarchy

Can you see how a WHY question is more confrontational than a WHAT question?

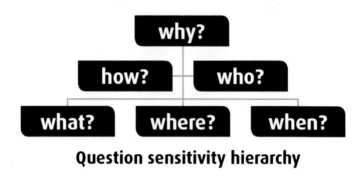

Question sensitivity hierarchy

- Ask a WHY question when emotions run high in a meeting and it's like throwing petrol onto a bonfire

- Ask a stranger a WHY question and you'll struggle to get a conversation going or will prompt a prickly response

Lower-tier questions are gentler, more enquiring, respectful and show genuine interest.

Try this on your spouse when they come downstairs ready to go out for the evening:

"Why are you wearing that colour shirt?"

Can you see how this could be somewhat incendiary? Like throwing a hand grenade into your evening!

You can be far less confrontational with a question from lower down the hierarchy to start the conversation:

> *"When did you get that shirt?"*

> *"Where did you buy that shirt?"*

> *"How formal is the evening?"*

When applied to a business conversation the same principles apply.

> *"Why do you believe talent is more important than repeating practice?"*

This challenging and confrontational question is likely to prompt a business owner to defend their point of view. It might undermine a relationship a little because WHY questions like this challenge people's opinions, attitudes and beliefs.

You can soften the question, make it more diagnostic and respectful by using questions from the bottom two layers like HOW or WHAT:

> *"How come you give more credence to talent than to practice?"*

> *"What is it that makes you think talent trumps practice?"*

These lower-tier questions are perceived to be more 'seeking to understand', respectful questions and less challenging than WHY questions.

You can thus better nurture the relationship with less sensitive questions and still get the answers you need to be a great Business Growth Accountant.

What's also neat is you'll discover that these lower-tier questions are easier to ask and easier for clients to answer.

One (question framework) for the road

Another great framework from the English sales training expert Neil Rackham is SPIN[34].

If you consider yourself a life-long learner about business, you'll certainly want to investigate the books, the audio programmes and the courses about the question framework SPIN:

S – SITUATION

P – PROBLEM

I – IMPLICATIONS

N – NEEDS/PAYOFF

Neil Rackham's framework suggests you ask questions about your client's situation. Like the earlier PJA framework, you also ask more pointed questions about

---

[34] *'SPIN Selling' by Neil Rackham*

your client's problem and the implications of inaction or consequences of changing something. And you also question your client about what they want and need and about the payoff they'll get or miss out on.

It's a framework worth investigating further.

Try this 'get out of jail' phrase too

Chapter 12 is entirely focused on habits, because your habits ultimately determine the outcomes of the life you lead, including your life as a Business Growth Accountant.

For example, your eating habits, your exercise habits and your question habits determine your weight, your health and your conversation (relationship building) skills respectively.

The key to installing new habits is to set up triggers or cues that prompt a behaviour.

There's a brilliant little two-word phrase that taps into your sub-conscious and encourages your brain to help find you a question worth asking. It triggers a question almost automatically.

Robert Cialdini in his landmark book on influence[35] would call it a 'click-whirr' phrase because when you use it (click)

---

[35] 'Influence – The Psychology Of Persuasion' by Robert Cialdini

your brain whirrs into action to give you a worthy question to ask

It's your two-word 'get out of jail' trigger phrase that's definitely worth practicing:

"Tell me..."

This phrase is your best friend whenever you're unsure of what question to ask. It's not an alternative to wholehearted preparation and practice but is useful if ever you get stuck.

Use 'tell me', then use one of the six question words (not WHY to be on the safe side!) and let your brain fill in the space...

Tell me, what...............?"

"Tell me...	"Tell me...	Now you try:
...**WHAT** do you think of our book's number 1 status on Amazon?"	...**HOW** big a difference will a 10% profit improvement make to you and your business?"	Tell me... ....

Practising the use of this click-whirr trigger – "Tell me, what..." – will build this simple but powerful questioning habit and skill.

"But what if they ask you a question?"

Steph Hinds of GrowthWise in Australia is also listening out for the questions her client asks:

> *"...it's listening to the questions that clients are asking and really being able to drill down into, what's the big underlying problem?*
>
> *And that comes from having really, really good skillsets of being able to listen and understanding fundamentals of a business and understanding the fundamental journeys that business owners go through as they're going from just starting, all the way through along that growth path and just really knowing where they're up to."*

One skill you should practice when clients ask you questions can be very useful when used carefully:

SKILL 1: Answer a question with a question

Losing control of a conversation can happen when a client starts asking all the questions. To resolve this, practice answering a question with a question.

Like this...

Question: "How can I increase sales across my higher margin products?"

Your answer: "That's a great question. Tell me, what have you done in the past that resulted in higher sales?"

(Please notice how it can help oil the wheels of conversation to compliment their question before replying with a question of your own)

Why not do a team exercise creating different answers (as a question) to the client question above?

Your answer:

Work with your team to generate a list of questions your clients often ask, so you can craft answers and craft questions you can use in reply.

Use these examples on your own or with your colleagues and build your skill of answering a question with a question. This can be a lot of fun!

Now for a real tough one:

Question: "I know my business better than you do so how can you successfully act as a business advisor to me?"

Your answer: "You're right, you know your business best. However, when have you visited a customer or supplier or any other business and, as an outsider, seen clearly how to improve their business?"

(Please notice how you repeat their question as a statement, then ask them how they would respond or have responded)

Why not do a team exercise creating different answers to the client question above?

Your answer:

And to help further – because you can't rely entirely on answering a question with a question – there's more learning needed.

There will come a time when you will have to share some knowledge, insight and experience and make a recommendation. How do you set yourself up for sharing such knowledge and insight?

Here's a short answer to a long (life-long) solution.

SKILL 2: Learn about a wide variety of business issues and insights in a deep way

Sounds like a big ask, I know...

...but don't despair at the scale of this strategy.

You already know so much.

Remember Steph Hinds thoughts on the value of clients asking questions:

> *"...it's listening to the questions that clients are asking and really being able to drill down into, what's the big underlying problem?*
>
> *And that comes from having really, really good skillsets of being able to listen and understanding fundamentals of a business and understanding the fundamental journeys that business owners go through as they're going from just starting, all the way through along that*

growth path and just really knowing where they're up to."

Steph is describing a process of listening to the questions business owners ask, as well as asking more questions about the big underlying problem behind their question.

Not just taking the question at face value.

In interviewing Steph, it was evident that she would see a client asking an awkward or difficult question as a learning moment.

This is a good thing if it then it prompts a little research, investigation and sharing with your colleagues – something I'm confident you'd see Steph do:

> *"...our passion at GrowthWise is just being able to solve problems. Over the years, we've kind of gathered all the problems that clients throw at us."*

> *Steph Hinds*

What Steph is describing above requires a knowledge of many businesses over many years.

You already have your life-long learning about your clients, plus additional learning from courses, books, online programmes, audio programmes. You have travelled many miles already on your life-long learning journey. You just have to keep going and continue to build your insight and knowledge.

It's what Luke Smith of Purpose refers to when he says:

"...basically, it comes down to knowing the theory..."

Luke is learning the theory not only so that when he shares the insights with clients they take him seriously, but also because he cares about them.

Just like Steph and her team genuinely care, as do all the Business Growth Accountants we interviewed.

Questions are the accountant's future

Kevin Kelly looks into the future and suggests what will shape the future of our lives and our business. In his book[36] 'The Inevitable', one of the 12 forces he puts forward is the power of questioning. Here's Kelly's definition of a good question:

"A good question is not concerned with a correct answer.

A good question challenges existing answers.

A good question is one you badly want answered once you hear it, but had no inkling you cared before it was asked.

---

[36] *'The Inevitable – Understanding The 12 Technological Forces That Will Shape Our Future' by Kevin Kelly*

A good question creates new territory of thinking.

A good question reframes its own answers.

A good question is the seed of innovation in science, technology, art, politics, and business.

A good question is a probe, a what-if scenario.

A good question skirts on the edge of what is known and not known, neither silly nor obvious.

A good question cannot be predicted.

A good question will be the sign of an educated mind.

A good question is one that generates many other good questions.

A good question may be the last job a machine will learn to do.

A good question is what humans are for."

Kevin Kelly, "The Inevitable"

Read that last line again as...

"A good question is what accountants are for."

In the world of business, I suggest that the last line points to your inevitable role as a Business Growth Accountant...

"A good question is what accountants are for."

8

Learning unlocks true value...

"I don't divide the world into the weak and the strong, or the successes and the failures ...I divide the world into the learners and non-learners."

Benjamin Barber, Sociologist

The previous chapter clearly shows that your success as a Business Growth Accountant depends significantly on your ability to ask the right question at the right time.

The quality of the questions you ask business owners will be influenced by the knowledge you have about business success.

Business success is a broad subject. But what's reassuring is the fact you already know more than you think you know.

Let me explain.

1. What's helpful immediately is your experience of running and managing your own accountancy business. Please don't underestimate this bank of knowledge, insight and experiences

2. What's also massively helpful is all the businesses you've visited and seen work well (and not so well). Very few people go and see as many different working businesses as you do. And even fewer get to 'look under the bonnet' like accountants do.

3. And by simply changing the conversation you have with the same clients over the next three, six or 12 months (by asking different, better, simple questions) you'll learn a whole lot more

You've already started...

What's great is that you've already started the learning process in earnest by pursuing accountancy as a career.

>   *"...in order to become a qualified accountant, to be a chartered accountant, you've actually got to be pretty smart. And if you do a little bit of homework, it doesn't take you long to become a*

*very effective advisor. I think the trusting side of
it is already there."*

- Ric Payne, Principa

But knowing accountancy isn't enough.

Over the interviews we did for this book a theme revealed
itself about the successful Business Growth Accountants:

*"...they have to be the sort of accountant that
sees it through a business owner's eyes...*

*...from a mindset perspective, they have to be
coming at it and seeing it from the business
owner's point of view, not theirs"*

What's clear is that a 9-to-5 employee compliance
accountant mindset is very different to the way business
owners work.

To be successful at Business Growth firms have to create
systems, processes, a culture and marketing, all supporting
a Business Growth Accountant's mindset within the firm.

Hence the point of making Advisory 1st and Accountancy
2nd in chapter 6.

Steph Hinds of GrowthWise sees training on the soft skills
as a priority and as a source of delivering value to clients
and even gaining a competitive advantage:

*"...every day I get better at questioning, every
day I get better at delivery and every day I get*

better at articulation, because it's the one thing that (me and my team) needs to improve in these skills.

Everyone in our organisation is actually really good at tax, they're really good from a technical standpoint and I think they're really good accountants.

So, all of our training that we're doing internally is focused on how to ask better questions, how to articulate things better, how to tell better stories, how to engage emotionally with clients and really how to just be human.

And I know that sounds really bizarre...

...but our training is focused on how to be human.

We (now) have a completely different skillset at GrowthWise than we ever have had before."

A back-to-school mindset

Every interviewee mentioned in some way, shape or form, the need for life-long learning about business success.

Yes, they'd learned to become qualified accountants.

They also learned about business success and now continue to learn about business success.

"If you're not learning, you're moving backwards."

Peter Taaffe, BWM Chartered Accountants

Learning about business success fuels the questions and conversations with clients. Learning also fuels the growth of their own Business Growth Accountancy firm.

Mundane accountant or magical advisor?

As a regular (and occasionally competitive) swimmer I was fascinated to read about Dan Chambliss, a sociologist, who completed a study of competitive swimmers titled "The Mundanity of Excellence." He observed that:

> *"...most stunning human achievements are the aggregate of countless individual elements, each of which on their own are ordinary.*
>
> *Greatness, he concluded, was doable no matter what your starting level of talent."*

Your success as a Business Growth Accountant is achievable no matter what your starting point. This is demonstrated by many comments from the business growth accountants who have contributed to this book...

...one reason the contributors to this book are successful at business advisory, at performing their chosen role as Business Growth Accountants, is due to their commitment to reading business books and attending workshops, webinars and courses on business, on sales, on marketing, on human resources, on leadership, on coaching, on systems and more.

> *"...we both worked our way through the audio tapes of a Jay Abraham[37] seminar in our cars, and for whatever reason we read The E-Myth[38] and we read a few other books... we attended Boot Camp[39]."*

This is Paul Kennedy again employing frameworks of learning he can use with his own firm and share with clients.

> *"...it's that mental framework of thinking of quality not quantity that I learnt at Boot Camp that probably set me on numerous journeys with numerous clients. But again, it's the mental framework, so education is everything."*

---

[37] *Jay Abraham is considered one of the world's most influential marketers. I can testify to the power of Jay's ideas having attended one of Jay's 4-day programmes. I've gone on to apply many of his concepts successfully to my businesses and to the accountancy firms I consult with.*

[38] *'The E Myth Revisited' by Michael Gerber.*

[39] *Boot Camp by RAN1 And RAS was a Ric Payne and Paul Dunn programme helping accountants develop a smarter approach to running and growing an accountancy firm, including better ways to work with clients.*

That last three words from Paul Kennedy's last statement are worth repeating

"education is everything"

Luke Smith of Purpose has a similar attitude towards learning:

"We have to earn the right to work with them (business owners) on their issues"

"...continuous learning is critical to asking best questions and providing insights."

"My kindle is rammed with business books. 5 years reading 1 book every month, 60 books."

Luke Smith, Purpose

Luke peppers our conversation with insights and stories from some of the world's best business books. You'll find some of Luke's favourites in the 'Read and Recommended' section at the end of this book.

Here's Aynsley Damery talking about his firm's commitment to education:

"We do quite a lot of training and we do quite a lot of development of the team, like the scaling-up workshop in Dublin with the senior advisory team, and we're always looking at outside business training like the Tony Robbins training, the business mastery, a couple of my senior team have been to.

> *But even internally, I've felt that maybe roleplays weren't enough for what we were doing so we're looking at trying to develop some weekly roleplays and weekly training and I think that's really, really important."*

An inspired step by Aynsley has been to join a business network and volunteer his team's time so they can be exposed to business owner thinking:

> *"...we've been asked to guest mentor on a range of masterminds for one business network...*
>
> *...having (our) guys having exposure to a day of business people asking questions of a group, and not having the pressure on them but having them there to input and to give advice when they feel comfortable, will just hugely increase and expand their comfort zone and their business understanding and questioning skills."*

Luke Smith, Rob Walsh, Andrew Botham, Aynsley Damery, Paul Kennedy, Greg Smargiassi, James Solomons and others commit to learning whilst running their accountancy practices. They read books, attend workshops and courses and invite experts into their firms.

Greg Smargiassi went a step further, several steps. Greg left accountancy (temporarily) and retrained:

> *"I joined an international coaching network and through that learnt a lot more about business beyond the numbers"*

"I think what people need to realise is that they have a certain skill set and a certain talent that gets them so far, but to improve the business they need to improve themselves"

Which is why one of Greg's most valued business books is:

'What Got You Here Won't Get You There' by Marshall Goldsmith

Why not treat the idea of learning better business advisory skills as a healthy dose of continuing professional development (CPD).

Then you too can develop the skills, insights, experiences and stories necessary to succeed at business advisory work. You've already got this book in your locker - what's next?

The concept – 'what's next' – is essential.

All the people we interviewed constantly seek out new knowledge, new experiences, new sources of inspiration and new learning. I never saw a once-a-year or once-a-quarter learning process from any of these people. It was constant and either a weekly or monthly obsession.

The Business Growth Accountants I interviewed never see Continuing Professional Development as a drag or as a necessary evil. They see it is a joy. Learning was and is a habit of successful Business Growth Accountants. The same goes for the ones I've met at the many events I've attended and presented at over the last 15 years.

This 'back-to-school mindset' shone through with every firm we interviewed:

"There has to be an 'I want to learn how to do this now' and that 'back-to-school' mindset that they want to grow and learn.

Are you building the learning habit? A learning obsession?

If you are, you're on the right track.

And what's massively reassuring is that the learning mindset drops perfectly into the growth mindset research of Carol Dweck and therefore signposts your future success.

Here's Peter Taaffe advocating a learning stance so that you remain valuable to your clients:

"I think keeping yourself challenged on what you can and can't advise on is so critical to this. If you retreat into traditional accountancy, the client is going to get bored fairly quickly as they realise, actually, you're not prepared to help."

Steph Hinds and her team at GrowthWise have seriously and deliberately built a learning habit. How could they not when their company strapline is:

"Think, Learn, Grow and Kick Arse"

For two hours, on 30 Fridays of the year, the whole team at GrowthWise get together and investigate asking better questions, better listening, better articulation of issues and better conversation management.

And Steph doesn't restrict learning to the 30 formal sessions (although formal isn't a word you'd use to describe Steph!):

> *"On top of that, I'll often do an impromptu role-playing session with people during the day, I use it as a good opportunity in the office to bring the mood up and to get everybody excited, if I know that everyone's flat on things that are more compliance and boring-driven, I'll often try and break that day up with, all right, here's a situation, let's role play that."*

> *"...it's also sharing important learnings, so for me, it'll be sharing important articles that other people have written or blog posts, books that are helpful for the team to learn as well, and I think that comes down to, as a business we know what we're trying to do, so we know what we're trying to deliver."*

Steph's commitment to "Think, Learn, Grow and Kick Arse" is taken deadly seriously by her and her team:

> *"...we have rules inside GrowthWise that if you're not contributing to our learning channel and slack every day, you're fired. It is a non-negotiable. Which means everyone in our office is thinking every day, everyone is learning every single day. We're learning from each other, we're learning from ourselves, we're learning from our clients."*

They also work with their clients with the same commitment to growing their clients' knowledge and business. They have a creative way of packaging and labelling their services:

> *"...we have our L-Platers, P-Platers and Black Ops, and there's Black Ops Junior and then full blown Black Ops. And we have one package on top of that which is a very high CFO based package where we are, effectively, sitting internally in their organisations, just not as a full-time staff member. So, we do have five packages."*

Smaller, recently-formed businesses get the equivalent of driving lessons on the L-plate and P-plate advisory packages. And, as the labels suggest, increasing depth is provided to more established and ambitious businesses on their 'Black-Ops' packages.

I can't recommend highly-enough that you read Steph's interview transcript to see fully how committed Steph and her team are to this learning approach. And lots of detail on how Steph makes it work. As a team they have built a very healthy 300+ client firm which is business advisory first and accountancy second.

You've got instant access to more learning as part of your investment in this book including Steph's whole interview at this URL – www.paulshrimpling.com/bga-resources and use this access code – **bga-resources2018** – to open the resources from this webpage.

An easy learning habit to start

If you want a small easy addition to your learning programme join our Business Bitesize mailing list – you'll then receive a 4-page easy-to-read (and easy-to-share) PDF report every two months.

Each report covers a business breakthrough worth taking seriously and applying to your firm, as well as worth sharing with your clients too.

You'll find various Business Bitesize reports peppered all over our business website at Remarkable Practice, particularly on our blog page...

http://www.remarkablepractice.com/blog.

Go take a look, click a blog you fancy the look of, then click a link to a Business Bitesize report you fancy and see what you can learn in the time it takes to drink a cup of tea.

Or if you want instant access to the Business Bitesize reports referenced in this book simply go to www.paulshrimpling.com/bga-resources and use this access code – **bga-resources2018** – to open the resources from this webpage. Or visit the shortened url http://bit.ly/2plWsea

9

Numbers to grow by

On the opening pages of this book I stated...

> *...the words you speak and the numbers you talk about can change the lives of your business owner clients.*

To demonstrate, here's how a simple number change can alter what people do as well as the results they get.

I recently refereed a practice match for my son's under-16s rugby team.

But I changed the scoring system.

- 1 point for a try scored (normally 5 points)

- 2 points for an offload (a pass to a teammate) within 10 metres of the try line if the try is scored

- 4 points for a second offload within 5 metres of the try line if the try is scored

By changing the scoring system, the boys changed their behaviour. Not immediately, but very quickly.

Instead of going for individual glory, the players were looking to offload the ball to a teammate.

Instead of lazily letting the speedsters score an individual try, other players were running in support to take the pass and get the extra points. Some even took the pass and looked to pass again to score maximum points.

As in sport, so in business.

Change the scoring system, change the numbers being measured and you'll change people's behaviour.

For scoring system, think KPIs.

So, let's talk KPIs – but not Key Performance Indicators.

Let's talk Key **PREDICTIVE** Indicators.

Key **PREDICTIVE** Indicators (numbers) can predict the future results of a business – partly because they change the way people behave, change what people do and how they do it and, as a result, change the results of the business.

Why would you shift from dealing in classic accountancy numbers to predictive KPIs?

Let's see how a conversation about KPIs worked for a business close to collapse...

A business survives then thrives...

When we interviewed Greg Smargiassi in Australia, he had just 16 business clients and the equivalent of £560,000 of advisory (Business Growth) fees.

Greg's £35,000[40] average fee looks like he knows how to market and price his work as a Business Growth Accountant.

But can he deliver?

---

[40] *In Greg's interview, he naturally quotes figures in Australian dollars valuing the business at A$6m. We used an exchange rate of £0.5 to A$1 You can read the full interview with Greg here – www.paulshrimpling.com/bga-resources and use this access code – **bga-resources2018** – to open the resources from this webpage. Or visit the shortened url http://bit.ly/2plWsea*

In a word, Yes. Greg helped drag a business owner back from the brink of business failure and liquidation...

...and when the same business owner, two years later, agreed a sale of 45% of the business to one of his customers for £1.35m (valuing the business at £3m)...

...the decision not to fold was so obviously the right one.

The business owner's decision to choose Greg and follow his guidance clearly paid off, big time.

The size of Greg's firm (only 16 clients) is irrelevant; the size of Greg's thinking is more relevant.

Actually, it's the clarity of Greg's thinking that stands out.

And Greg's focus on using a framework of three numbers helped this business client survive and then went on to help the same business thrive.

Just like the rugby example at the beginning of this chapter, Greg helped the business owner focus on *different numbers* and got *different actions*. The different numbers and different actions turned a business on the edge of extinction into a valuable asset for the owners.

Your firm, any firm, can obsess about the right numbers, just like Greg.

Greg simply hunts down accurate and relevant numbers for the business's success.

You can go hunting for Key Predictive Indicators too.

More on Greg's three key metrics in a moment.

'Now-focused' numbers

The simple shift to looking at current (rather than historical) numbers can be transformative.

Cloud accounting helps you do this with clients.

Jonathan Myers, of the firm UWM in Leeds, works with Martin who runs a 20-year-old, 3-site bar business. Because they changed the accessibility of the KPIs for their managers they tripled the profits of the business.

Martin (with Jonathan's help) put the KPIs of the business in the hands of all the managers across the three bars – updating financial dashboards every day (using Futrli) helping them make better, more timely, decisions.

Because they changed the accessibility of the KPIs for their three-site business, they tripled the profits of the business.

All because they gave their bar managers 'timely' access to the performance of their bar. Seeing the current, just-happened numbers drove better decisions and better actions.

Just like changing the numbers did in the U16s rugby game.

You can go hunting for now-focused numbers too. You can go hunting for future-focused numbers as well...

'Future-focused' numbers pay off

Greg Smargiassi uses a three-part framework around which he questions and supports his advisory clients:

> *"...accountants normally look in the rear-view mirror, we teach people how to visualise their future using numbers and visual tools."*

> *"And there are three key metrics you must absolutely understand about your business before you build strategy around your business."*

More on Greg's three key metrics coming up.

Let's just stick with the driving metaphor for a moment.

When you think about it, you instantly know how hard it is to drive a car whilst only looking in the rear-view mirror.

It's equally hard to steer a business by looking at historical numbers.

Yes, the past numbers are source of valuable information, but only if they are timely.

What cloud accounting allows you to do is look at timely numbers.

Cloud technology also makes the creation of KPI dashboards easier so that you can help your clients predict the future performance of their business.

But does all this mean anything to your business-owner clients?

If the numbers drive action like the rugby scoring numbers drive action, like Greg's three numbers drive action, then yes, the right future focused (or predictive) numbers can be your way of influencing the behaviour, the actions and the results of your business-owner clients.

Now you can start to see how Greg Smargiassi, Luke Smith, Rob Walsh and Andrew Botham (numbers experts like you) confidently charge £35,000, £24,000, £18,000 for a future focused numbers conversation that their clients value.

By shifting your questions with business owners from old numbers to future numbers you change the conversation.

Most accountants look backwards. Most accountants discuss old numbers – annual accounts, management accounts, tax to pay, etc.

There is so much more value to be given by looking to the future rather than in looking in the rear-view mirror all the time.

Measure what matters most

A great way to look at KPIs (predictive) is by looking at what matters to your customers.

Ron Baker's suggestions[41] on this point to the value of predictive rather than performance indicators. So why not quiz your clients on:

-   The bespoke Key Predictive Indicators that are the most important measures for your business-owner client.

-   Input measures rather than output measures.

-   Activity numbers rather than results.

'Key Performance Indicators' become *'Key Predictive Indicators'*. Your KPIs become a business canary!

Canary-like KPIs

You may know why miners used to take canaries down the mine with them...

To predict their future survival!

Should a canary stop singing and fall off its perch, the miners knew the air quality was dangerous.

But here's what matters most about this story...

---

[41] *'Measure What Matters To Your Customer' by Ron Baker. I think this book is a classic and even though it's hard to find a copy, it's worth the search (and the price you'll have to pay!).*

13 minutes if you're lucky!

The emergency breathing equipment the miners used had between six and thirteen minutes of air. So, when a canary fell off its perch, miners were fast to put on their breathing masks. Then they legged it – they got out of there fast!

Consequences of inaction were clear and obvious.

Action happened quickly and decisively.

The consequence of action or inaction was to live or die.

The consequences are less cut and dried or obvious or critical in business but measuring the right predictive numbers can help your clients see what's going to happen.

Help your clients act fast (like the miners did) when these *'Key **Predictive** Indicators'* change and business success is more likely. Do this and you'll be on the road to becoming a successful and trusted Business Growth Accountant.

Business Growth Accountants are also numbers obsessed

You learned earlier about the importance, the value and the necessity for life-long learning.

Well, as an accountant you've been learning about numbers all your working life. You're a numbers master already.

But just like Roger Federer, who built a long and successful tennis career, you have to learn more and practice more to stay at the top.

Greg Smargiassi appreciates this which is why, on developing the service offering for his OurCFO business, he went back to school!

> *"I researched and understood what a CFO does in big organisations and then developed our processes to see how we could deliver that external to businesses."*

Which brings us to **Greg's three sets of numbers** that underpin his OurCFO firm.

> *"...what we've done is build a visual representation of, what I call, the financial structure.*
>
> *"The three elements are profitability, cashflow and financial position."*

Greg uses what initially sound like old-style classic numbers reports to help drive client behaviour, with the exception of one he calls 'the meth report'.

Meth is a label used in Australia for the narcotic amyl nitrate also known as poppers. This is a drug that warps a person's reality. And in Greg's experience, business owners rarely see the reality of the cash, profit and capital value of their business. So, Greg helps them see that reality.

Plus, he helps drive the right behaviours by making it simple for his clients:

"How can I make this so simple that the client understands it and they can educate themselves, then they can do a strategy and then they can have the confidence to make decisions and move forward."

Greg's desire and follow-through action to make it easy and simple for clients to see and understand their financial position is to be applauded. And giving clients clarity clearly delivers value based on the success Greg is achieving.

But could even greater value be delivered with genuinely predictive indicators?

As Ron Baker points out, in a recent email conversation, that:

"...profit and cash flow are lagging (unless cash flow is a projection) not predictive indicators... You'll never be able to pull predictive indicators off a financial statement, even from a cloud based, real-time (system). Cloud elevates from lagging to coincidental indicators, but not leading."

Start at home

I asked Paul Dunn 'what other behaviours or beliefs do you think distinguish the most effective and successful business advisory accountants from the others?'

"...that they walk-the-talk. They walk-the-talk in terms of the measures, the KPIs that they work with. And everybody on the team is working with those KPIs. And those KPIs become client-centred KPIs."

Paul's walk-the-talk comment also came through in the interview with Luke Smith, Rob Walsh and others.

If you set out to talk KPIs with your clients, you had better be measuring and acting on the KPIs for your own firm. To be a genuine advisor or Business Growth Accountant you cannot have cobbler's shoes (with holes!).

You've got to obsess about the right 'client-centred' KPIs for your own firm[42] as well as for your clients.

So which KPIs should your firm be measuring?

Here's an (almost) ancient 20th century story to capture the power of measuring what matters to the customer.

---

[42] *For a list of the KPIs that I've seen work in the dozens of accountancy firms and thousands of meetings I've conducted over the last 15 year,s go to www.paulshrimpling.com/bga-resources. Use this access code – **bga-resources2018** – to open the resources from this webpage. These KPIs have helped accountants improve their firms' fees, profits, cash and capital value. Or visit the shortened url http://bit.ly/2plWsea*

Use customer-focused KPIs

In 1994, Continental Airlines was failing miserably. In the previous decade, it had filed for bankruptcy twice. But then Gordon Bethune took over.

Continental had a complex set of measures for their business, mostly focused on cost reduction – so Bethune theatrically burned the employee rulebook in their car park to make a point...

...the rules had changed!

Instead of the cost-focused measures, Bethune simply got every employee focused on three ***customer-focused KPIs***.

Together they delivered a remarkable comeback - Continental became one of the most profitable airlines in the sky by the late 1990s[43].

The game changed because Bethune changed the KPIs.

He dumped all the complex cost focused measures and got every employee focused on the following three customer-focused KPIs:

1) Less lost luggage

---

[43] *For a full review of the Continental Airlines turnaround check out this Harvard Business Review article -*
https://hbr.org/1998/09/right-away-and-all-at-once-how-we-saved-continental *Or the book 'From Worst To First' by Gordon Bethune. Visit* http://bit.ly/2HLFYUe *for the shortened url.*

2) Fewer complaints

3) More on-time arrival

Notice how all three KPIs *matter to their customers*.

Profits soared because they focused on KPIs that made a dramatic difference to the way their people behaved.

Bethune got all Continental employees to take regular action to improve these three customer-focused KPIs.

Next, here's a story from Andrew Botham, a Business Growth Accountant obsessed about customer-focused KPIs.

Robust KPI systems keep Aldi happy

Andrew Botham's firm, Mayes Accountancy, works out of a small and very humble Lancashire town called Accrington.

The story captures the whole process of how any accountant can manage a conversation by using KPIs with a client.

Rather than isolate specific quotes, here's a section of our interview that describes exactly how Andrew makes the KPI conversation work with a client[44].

---

44 *This interview with Andrew Botham was conducted on stage in front of an audience of accountants and so not all questions are from Paul – you can get the transcript of the full interview here –*

Look out for the detail on the KPIs that matters to the customer.

Paul   So what difficulties or challenges do you have getting the clients, the business owners, to identify these KPIs?

Andrew   Well, there's a raft of challenges there. It's probably one of the most difficult aspects of the whole process. Clients only want to track what they can easily track, so they've got Xero or Sage or whatever, they've got a CRM system or whatever they use for internal controls for things, and they want to track stuff they've already got coming out of these systems. But when we have the conversations, invariably, the things we need to track, they've got no measures in place within the business in order to track it.

So, the most challenging aspect of the whole process is to get the clients to understand the importance of putting together a very simple but robust series of systems in order to track three or four or five measures that need to go onto the plan that they haven't got systems in place for. And they're invariably the ones that

_____

www.paulshrimpling.com/bga-resources and use this access code – **bga-resources2018** – to open the resources from this webpage. The shortened url is _http://bit.ly/2plWsea_

are actually going to change – transform – the business results.

*So I call those **robust underlying systems** because, unless they're robust, what we're tracking on the Business One Page Plan is not accurate. And if it's not accurate, it's meaningless.*

It's a bit like what we were talking about earlier, results in your practice. If you didn't know exactly when you needed to do the work and who was going to do it and how it was planned out, and you were guessing, then it just wouldn't have any meaning. So it's exactly the same.

We've got a company who are industrial floor cleaners, and they work with the likes of Aldi and Lidl and fairly big retail companies. Their biggest problem was that it took several days, when a machine broke down at Aldi, for one of their engineers to go out and fix it. And when they went out to fix it, invariably, they didn't fix it the first time. They didn't have the right parts, or they hadn't been given the right instructions by the client as to what the challenge was.

So we put two measures in on the Business One Page Plan (BOPP), under the success predictors section of the BOPP[45]. One was the first fix

---

[45] *You can find out more about Andrew's proprietary KPI tool BOPP here - https://www.businessonepageplan.co.uk/*

ratio, and the other was the time it took to fix. The client didn't have that information to hand. They knew it was a problem, they knew that invariably customers would complain that it took a long time to get to them and then it wasn't fixed the first time, but they didn't know the expense of it.

So, we helped them build a very simple Excel spreadsheet, number of customers, the dates, couple of formulas in there – which accountants can do, so it's not something that's difficult for us to do. And we said, here we are, get your admin lady to populate this every single day, and I'll see what it looks like. And it was horrible, it really was horrible. They were really making a mess of it. It was over a week on average for them to get things fixed, and about 70% of the time, it wasn't fixed the first time.

Now, a few years later, about 80% of the time it is fixed first time, and it's fixed on the same day. So just putting those two measures into play in the company made a massive difference.

Paul   Driven a load of action.

Andrew   Well, those are two things that they would never have thought of tracking and didn't have a system to track. But it's transformed the customer experience for all their customers. Moments of truth.

Paul   *So you or your team built this Excel file as an extra fee, or as part of the Business One Page Plan?*

Andrew   *Within the £1,050 a meeting[46]. It took a fairly junior member of the team an hour to build it. I'm not going to charge for that, you know. Little bits like that, if you can add those in because you've got the skillset within the practice... It just adds to that relationship, building up the relationship. And it feels very valuable to them, because they don't have to do it.*

Person B   *Can I ask, how did the problem on machines... How did that come out in conversation? Was it something specific you asked?*

Andrew   *Yes. The first step is to ask about the goals, where they want to go. The second step is, what do you think the challenges are in your business? What problems and issues? And he said, well, we're having a lot of complaints about the time it's taking to fix the machinery.*

What would Aldi and Lidl have done if Andrew's client had not fixed the problems described above?

Chances are they'd have been tempted to take their business elsewhere.

---

[46] *You'll find more on pricing in the pricing Chapter 11*

Andrew's conversation, the clarity and focus on two simple KPIs, and the decisions and actions that followed helped this business keep valuable contracts and secure the future of the business.

All thanks to their KPI-obsessed accountant.

Steph Hinds runs GrowthWise in Newcastle, Australia, also with very much an 'advisory first, accountancy second' approach.

Steph talks about access to good timely data thanks to robust systems as well, but accountancy systems:

> *"...when I started my career 18 years ago, we just didn't have access to data and that was a problem as an accountant, you didn't have access to really, really good data. Today, my data doesn't necessarily come from accounting programmes, my data comes from point of sale programmes for clients or from their inventory software of from their CRM software or a combination of all of those things."*

Steph and her team are doing what Andrew Botham and Greg Smargiassi are doing. They:

- Help clients access good timely business intelligence

- Help clients set up robust systems for the right KPIs

And to use Steph's preferred language, they:

- 'Kick arse' and help clients take the decisions and action necessary to grow their business

Aynsley Damery when discussing KPIs used to talk 'strategic planning' with clients but Aynsley felt this was too much for clients with modest-sized business. So Aynsley changed and simplified the language he uses:

> *"KPIs are fundamental...*
>
> *...for our clients we really encourage them to do a financial modelling day with us.*
>
> *"...in the financial model we're actually saying really what's possible with the business. We're not looking at the past, although it is helpful and a good starting point. We're actually really trying to say to people what's possible within your business.*
>
> *And when we drill it down and get into the activities that generate those results, that's where we can really, really find that we can get some really interesting performance indicators."*

Rocket scientists need not apply

What Andrew and Steph and Aynsley describe in their interviews are simple conversations. Simple conversations using some simple, obvious and even occasionally, dumb questions. Questions that result in a meaningful conversation with a client. A conversation the client values because it transforms the results of their business and the way they feel.

1. A question or two about the business owner's future goals – can't any accountant ask these?

2. A question or two about the challenges or difficulties the business is experiencing, which any and every accountant could also ask

3. And then a discussion about measuring the numbers on a customer-focused KPI that drives decisions and actions

Can you see how rocket scientists need not apply?

All three are conversations most business owners would appreciate having with their accountant.

All three are conversations any and every accountant can have with a business-owner client.

In fact, all three are conversations business owners would EXPECT to have with an accountant that genuinely cared about their business!

Making use of this insight means putting it to work. Work at using the basic questions above and see how it changes the dynamic, the value and the quality of the conversation you have with your client.

It's up to you to make it happen...

> *"Perhaps the most valuable result of all*
> *education is the ability to make yourself do the*

thing you have to do, when it ought to be done, whether you like it or not.

It is the first lesson that ought to be learned and however early a person's training begins, it is probably the last lesson a person learns thoroughly."

Thomas Henry Huxley[47]

Make predictive KPIs your bread and butter!

Why not start a conversation about the numbers that matter to a client's customers?

Here's an exercise you could do, as a learning process for you or your management team.

Start by choosing an easy example.

---

[47] *https://en.wikipedia.org/wiki/Thomas_Henry_Huxley - an English biologist known as "Darwin's Bulldog" for his advocacy of Charles Darwin's theory of evolution. For the shortened url visit http://bit.ly/2GJv9Ta*

Think of a restaurant client that you may have, since most of your team eat in restaurants and they may have experienced issues as a customer.

1. Start by working out what issues the restaurant might be having with less-than-happy customers?

2. Think about the Key Predictive Indicators that might be worth tracking on these issues

3. Identify robust systems that could be used to help the restaurateur measure these KPIs

4. Work out what questions you could ask your restaurateur about these numbers

This might seem challenging at first and might throw up some numbers that are hard to measure.

For example, it's easy to ascertain the exact cost of the meal, but it can be difficult to get an accurate measure of customer satisfaction. Customer satisfaction, however, is a very strong predictive indicator for the success of any restaurant.

As Ron Baker[48] suggests:

---

[48] 'Measure What Matters To Customers' by Ron Baker is one of the definitive all-time great books on KPIs. Print copies are hard to get but Ron tells me the book is still available 'print-on-demand' from the USA publisher and a kindle edition can also be obtained.

> *"Exact measurements of the wrong things can drive out good judgements of the right things."*

Your business owners will value knowing, with a greater sense of certainty, how their business is performing. They'll also appreciate knowing how well their business will perform in the future – and that's the value of Key Predictive Indicators.

As the numbers expert, you're already well placed to ask questions about numbers, and your clients expect it.

Why not build a conversation and reach agreement on how to best identify and use predictive indicators with your clients, perhaps even charging for such a high-value conversation, just as Andrew Botham of Mayes Accountancy has done for more than a decade! And just like Aynsley Damery does too:

> *"KPIs are massive because clearly if you can have three numbers which you can look at on a daily or monthly basis or weekly basis and know with certainty that as long as those three numbers are going the right way then you're going to make money then that's a fantastic way to run your business."*

Notice Aynsley is talking about three KPIs.

Greg Smargiassi was obsessed with just three numbers too.

Less is more...

Having worked with Andrew Botham for many years I have seen how successful he has been at talking KPIs with all types and sizes of business.

This narrowing of focus has been a big part of the success Andrew's clients have achieved (thanks to Andrew's help).

Sifting the wheat from the chaff is your job as a Business Growth Accountant.

> *"...we're dealing with 12 KPIs but we're only really focusing on two or three of them. But we're reporting on 12.*
>
> *I simplify stuff. I suppose, that's everything I do, in the way I speak and the way I talk to people about what it is. But also in how I report back, it's the simple... you know, the old keep it simple kind of rule."*
>
> *Amanda Fisher, CFO and Business Mentor*

The value lies in identifying a handful of KPIs. And a handful of robust systems to make sure the KEY predictive indicators show up and help decision making.

You want your business clients to succeed. So...

...start talking to them about measuring a handful of Key Predictive Indicators.

...ask questions about their current KPIs. Questions about KPIs that matter to their customers. Questions about the systems they use to capture and report the KPIs.

10

Set your firm's stall out

> *"The better you are at marketing, the better the chance you have to work on fun stuff, and less trapped you become in being forced to take on work and clients you don't truly enjoy."*
>
> *David Maister from 'True Professionalism'*

To be successful at marketing your firm, you have to set your stall out.

To successfully set your firm's stall out you have to make a promise to your clients and prospects.

The firms interviewed for this book have all set out their stalls as Business Growth Accountants.

And the fact that you're reading this book, and have got this far, suggests you want to do the same.

When you become a Business Growth Accountant, you're letting yourself in for a strategic competitive advantage.

> *"I could count two, three firms that are doing it very well. I think you hit the nail on the head in terms of the word that you use around deliberate – having a 'deliberate' intent to deliver advisory services."*

This is a comment from Alex Davis. Alex is part of the business development team at Intuit and he spends most of his time speaking and consulting with the top 100 accounting firms in the UK.

Alex suggests there's a real desire to become advisory and generate the healthy fees advisory can provide, but it seems firms drop into two camps.

I asked Alex how many firms are making the leap to become a deliberate advisory firm:

> *"...firms will either make a panic reaction to what's happening (when they) see the commoditisation of compliance work and the squeeze on those kind of costs and then move straight to advisory and sign up to the latest piece of software that will allow them to produce the advisory boards and allow them to share KPIs and benchmarking data and that kind of thing, and immediately assume that means that they're now in the advisory space..."*

Alex goes on to describe the way other firms deliberately set their stall out as Business Growth Accountants:

> *"... (other firms) are very deliberate with the intent around advisory and completely shift their mindset to 'How can I sit down and not have time-based conversations with clients, not be looking at the watch, and actually being able to understand the pressures, the challenges and everything that those (business owners) are under?' And then look at tailored solutions to be able to essentially look after those business needs."*

Here Alex is talking about the top 100 UK firms which are committed, well-planned and deliberate in their approach to advisory. These firms are focused on the business owner's experience.

We didn't get chance to interview South Australian firm Perks[49] but comments by the team at Futrli (who work with Perks) suggested their approach looks like this:

> *"...we don't want to spend time with our clients, giving them an education lesson in the finances. We want to be able to speed through that and make sure that we've all got the same understanding. If there are any gaps we need to fill, let's do that quickly, but, really, we want to devote our time to explaining not what the*

---

[49] *https://www.perks.com.au/*

> *figures portray, but, 'What can we do about them?'"*

Cloud accounting and tools such as QuickBooks and Futrli free up time for higher value conversations with clients. But the tools are just one element.

As Alex Davis suggests, it's not the tactic of merely using a cloud advisory tool, but the cultural 'set-out-your-stall' commitment to advisory systems, processes, marketing and people that matters.

Your commitment to delivering Business Growth Accountancy is relevant to your people in your team too. Here are the thoughts from Peter Taaffe of BWM Chartered Accountants on attracting high-quality people and keeping them in his 60-strong team:

> *"...we're looking for bright and motivated individuals who are looking for quality of work, quality of experience, and career path.*
>
> *...they have to see and be enthused by the quality of the work that you're doing, and they will be involved with.*
>
> *That can be a key differentiator."*

At the core of your marketing success?

You have to deliver what you promise.

Especially if you're to maintain and grow your reputation as a trusted advisor.

Like Aynsley Damery of Tayabali Tomlin clearly states:

> *"...you can get clients in the door but if you're not delivering then they're not going to stay."*

Marketing and selling a promise which you fail to deliver will undermine your firm's credibility, reliability and trust.

If you fail to deliver on what you promise, you'll lose trust. Lose trust and you'll lose clients, lose fees, lose profits and lose capital value.

Reliability and credibility are important components of the trust equation.

Successful delivery must sit right at the core of your firm's marketing and selling. How could it not?

As an example, here's a case study from Andrew Price. Andrew runs a modest-sized firm in Torquay (Andrew Price & Co[50]) but has very high standards and a focus on helping his clients grow. On a recent call, Andrew described the progress one of his clients has made:

> *"Together we set a 12-month goal. For the business to jump from £200,000 net profit to £400,000 net profit by December 2016.*

---

[50] *www.andrewprice.co.uk*

235

Using 21 KPIs agreed with the client we built a forecast showing the delivery of the net profit growth over 52 weeks.

The client shares the weekly numbers, and my team update the excel and the graphs and shares them with the client. This prompts our client to take action to influence the KPIs.

Year ending 2016 the client achieved £401,000 of net profit.

We then set a target of £600,000 for December 2017 and ran the same process. The business was £50,000 short but £550,000 is a win non-the-less.

We're working with the owner to apply a similar process this year."

Remember Greg Smargiassi's client success story? A business on the brink of extinction turned into a 45% equity sale for £1.35m (see start of chapter 9).

The best marketing tells stories.

Emotional stories.

Success stories.

Stories are valuable because they generate strong feelings.

When you have played a major part in a business owner's success, you're going to be proud of the work you do. You're going to be more confident the next time you need to ask a challenging question of a client. You're going to believe deeply that what you know is of life-changing value to business owners.

And I'd suggest you aren't going to struggle to get recommendations to other business owners for more work as a Business Growth Accountant. You'll also find it easier to retain and recruit the best people for your firm.

Winning business growth client work

Most business owners, when making a big decision about investing time and money in your Business Growth Accountancy service, will need proof. They'll need evidence that you can deliver value as a Business Growth Accountant.

This can come in the form of case studies about businesses you've helped, testimonials from the same business owners, statistical evidence about the results you and your firm deliver and money-back guarantees.

All four forms of evidence reassure business owners and build confidence in your ability to deliver.

But one form of evidence trumps all of these 'vicarious' forms of evidence! *The test drive*.

Prove that you can deliver by providing a road test.

The 'alerts' within the reporting software (like Futrli) give you the ways and means to prove you are truly valuable.

Here's how the team at Futrli described an accountant's experience of doing just that. More through luck than judgement, but it worked and turned a A$1000 (£500) client into a A$12,000 (£6,000) client:

> *"He tried telling a client that he wanted to be his advisor, and it didn't really go down very well, even though he could see some really serious problems within this person's business."*

> *"So, what he did was go, 'Hang on a minute. I've done the research now. I've created a forecast. I've had a play around with this client. What I'm going to do is set some alerts up.'"*

The use of alerts created an opportunity to discuss pressing issues with this business owner. These conversations prompted decisions and action that helped the business. The accountant earned the right to higher fees by helping the business owner 'road test' his firm as a Business Growth Accountant.

Real evidence, not vicarious evidence.

He set his stall out as an advisor – made a promise.

He delivered against his promise before being paid.

He then agreed healthy fees to continue delivering against his Business Growth Accountancy promise.

Here's Amanda Fisher touching on the 'test drive' idea in a meeting with a prospect:

> *"...there is a school of thought that says you should never give away any information in the first meeting until they pay for it.*
>
> *If you're sitting there and you're in pain or whatever that is. It's business and let's just say, your cash flow is just a complete disaster. You know, it's no skin off my nose to say, have you done this and have you done that, have you thought about this. And then when you start to get the, oh, I hadn't thought about that then well, okay, why don't you... the first thing I would do is do this, this, this and this because that's going to really help. You know? And you just do it.*
>
> *...it's not about saying, well, if you want any answers, you've got to pay me and then I'll start talking to you."*

I agree with Amanda and actively seek to share something of significant value in meeting one with an accountancy firm. My goal is deliver something that would justify a year's worth of working with me.

What goes around comes around in my view and I think it's what Amanda is suggesting here:

> *"You just start to get a bit of a reputation as someone who will go out of her way to help and provide advice, even if there's no money on the table. And then when they really need it, it's kind*

of a no brainer to say, hey Amanda, can we have a conversation please."

Get started

Your journey as a Business Growth Accountant starts with helping your first client.

It starts by asking them better questions, agreeing KPIs that matter to their customers, helping them make a few key decisions and, perhaps, checking in on their action implementation. See them get going.

Then, start again with two more clients.

With some skills, knowledge, insights and a few errors behind you, you start to look at actively marketing and scaling your Business Growth approach.

Your marketing becomes credible because you have stories to tell, insights to share and knowledge to apply to prove you're the real deal.

For a deeper insight into how to use proof to enhance your firm's marketing, check out the free 4-page Business Bitesize report on the resources webpage here – www.paulshrimpling.com/bga-resources Use this access code – **bga-resources2018** – to open the resources from this webpage. For the shortened url see http://bit.ly/2plWsea

And next, what about scaling your Business Growth Accountancy service? You will need capacity, time, resources, people...

Capacity first, growth second

When we set up Remarkable Practice over a decade ago, we believed we'd be mostly helping firms improve their marketing and sales results.

It didn't work out quite as we'd planned, mainly because most firms are short on resources or use those resources ineffectively and inefficiently.

It makes no sense to install a sales and marketing programme when a firm can't cope with the existing work, never mind additional new work.

The same must be applied to becoming a Business Growth Accountant. How can you install new advisory ways of working if you can't cope with the existing accounts work?

Peter Taaffe of BWM Chartered Accountants makes this point well:

> *"Carving out time to deal with (advisory work) from a normal day job, because it does require time to build and it does require time flexibility to respond to a demand."*

Peter is suggesting you need capacity before you can build an advisory service across your firm.

Because trust is at the centre of the relationship between business owner and accountant, we've ended up investing more than half our efforts in helping accounting firms improve their ability to do the accountancy work faster without recruiting more people.

So, I have found myself using my production planning experience, acquired from running an upholstery company for more than a decade.

I use this weekly production obsession to help firms produce more work with the same or fewer people.

Strange as it may sound, producing four handmade-sofas a day, 20 a week, 80 a month, 240 a quarter, provides some deeply practical and relevant insights into turning round quarterly accounts jobs for all your clients.

Your capacity game changer

You now have a game changer at your disposal. Two, actually. Both deserve your attention.

Firstly, what's really exciting are the opportunities that cloud accounting and the support apps allow you to exploit.

Used well, cloud accounting frees up time across your firm.

Then, throw outsourcing into your plan and capacity goes up again.

It's how Nick Price[51] can deliver the best part of £400,000 worth of fee work with a part-time PA and a full-time chartered accountant – that's it!

What's Nick's secret?

Nick is good at pricing. Nick is wholeheartedly committed to outsourcing as much tax and accounts work as he can. Nick is committed to using cloud accounting. And Nick seeks out opportunities to help his clients be more successful, more cash rich, more profitable. In his own enigmatic fashion, Nick is a Business Growth Accountant.

What Nick has done by using both the cloud and outsourcing is build adaptive capacity in his firm.

Nick is using this adaptive capacity to grow his firm further by helping more of his existing clients and by marketing for new clients as well. He has the time to do this and the money to invest in marketing. He also has the capacity to do the extra work he will win.

Put adaptive capacity to work

Adaptive capacity ebbs and flows in your firm as it does in all firms.

You notice the lack of adaptive capacity during tax return season, holiday season or exam season. During these times,

---

[51] *Nick runs an independent and elegant firm in Harrogate, Yorkshire. At the time of writing the firm was called EuraAudit Harrogate but the name is soon to change.*

you find it harder to respond to extra work from important clients and find it harder to keep on top of your strategic projects.

If you and your people are busy all the time, special projects cease to see the light of day – they get lost in the melee of running a very busy practice. And when extra work gets done for clients, the billing process sometimes fails to happen and you don't get paid!

Instead, why not actively put better technology, process improvements, outsourcing and improvements in job and time planning to work in your firm?

With the adaptive capacity available, you can deliberately seek a competitive advantage for your firm and set your stall out as a genuine Business Growth Accountant.

Baker's law

It was great to spend a little time with Ron Baker recently and revisit the importance of adaptive capacity.

Ron brilliantly states the blindingly obvious – but something most firms fail to apply:

"Bad customers drive out good customers"

I've seen many firms, when faced with a choice between hitting a filing deadline for a low-grade client or doing a piece of urgent special work for a grade-A client, focus on hitting the filing deadline.

This choice is unnecessary if you have adaptive capacity built into your production plan – you can do both.

However, stop winning work with non-ideal clients (and consider removing some of your existing non-ideal clients) and you'll build adaptive capacity faster.

Check out Ron Baker's thoughts in the article below[52]. You'll see the way hotels and airlines create or ensure they always have adaptive capacity.

Embrace the idea of building adaptive capacity and your firm can adapt to whatever is most important:

- **Change-management projects** – converting clients from desktop accounting to cloud accounting, for example

- **Marketing projects** – finding and winning new clients that fit your ideal client profile

- **Responding to the urgent needs of 'grade-A' clients** so that they continue to be loyal to you and your firm

Adaptive capacity also creates the opportunity to make the most of your people. Not chasing filing deadlines because

---

[52] *Ron Baker in this post – http://verasage.com/blog/pricing-on-purpose/bakers_law_bad_customers_drive_out_good_custom ers/ – makes adaptive capacity a no-brainer production planning goal when you see the impact on an airline's approach to (not) filling all the seats in first class. The shortened url is http://bit.ly/2G3u9LR*

you have 'slack in your system' means you can invest in your best people and give them a sense of career progression so that they stay with you.

When you successfully retain and recruit the best people, with a Business Growth Accountancy approach, you enhance your competitive advantage.

So how do you make more of your people?

Leverage your team

Scaling for Business Growth Accountancy is a challenge.

It's especially challenging when you're embedded in an annual accounts and a desktop bookkeeping mindset.

Therefore, it's essential you use the technology at your disposal.

Cloud accounting will almost certainly make scaling BOTH accounts work and advisory work easier and more likely.

Using the technology to free up time for you and your team is a great first step (building adaptive capacity). But freeing time isn't enough.

The team at Futrli shared a few ideas based on what larger firms, like Perks in Australia are doing:

1. Promote your successes internally

Share results of case studies within your own firm. When you see a client's fees increase from £1900 to

£8100, it's easy to appreciate the value of Business Growth work.

Your people will respond well when you show how your work pays off for your business owners in increased profits, revenue growth, capital value growth and cash flow improvements.

The proof you use to demonstrate to business owners that you can and do help businesses grow can be used to educate your team as well.

2. Build workflows, processes and training for delivering advisory work

You'll find that the 'stars' – the people in your firm who are naturally suited to Business Growth work – don't necessarily know how they do what they do. They need help to work it out, to process map what they do.

Doing it on the fly works for the 'stars', but to scale the process across the firm you need a process to follow, tools to use and training.

3. Make Business Growth an intrinsic part of your firm

This means you should be seen as an advisory firm by everyone in your firm, as well as by clients. Your reception, social media, email marketing, website, client meetings and team meetings should all reflect your firm's Business Growth approach. Business Growth is who you are and what you do – the culture of the firm is advisory, business transformation, business growth.

> *"It's not just about the partner making the decision, it has to work all the way down to the project leads and then the worker bees who are actually preparing the numbers for the client. Get them involved, it shouldn't just be partner-led. This is fun, it's interesting, it's more fun that preparing a tax return."*

> *Hannah Dawson, Founder of Futrli*

But without something to **ENSURE** you have regular Business Growth conversations with clients, it will all be for nothing. You and your firm have to follow through on your advisory, business growth promises.

And the one suggestion from my conversation with Hannah Dawson, that I think profoundly improves the relationship you have with your clients is:

4. Have a conversation around alerts for the business

This aspect of the technology now at your disposal is profoundly powerful. It's so powerful because automated alerts perfectly tap into the neuroscience of forming habits (more on this in chapter 12).

One of the key things that you can do as an advisor (using products like Futrli) is to set up alerts.

You use alerts to prompt an email to you or your client or both of you when key metrics are hit. Metrics like cash position, profitability target, revenue target, or even how long it's taking your customers to pay you.

Such alerts enable you (and your client) to look at what thresholds within the business are acceptable and what's not. This prompts valuable conversations about the thresholds you choose together. Then the alerts trigger conversations with clients about successes or areas of concern.

Why is this so profoundly powerful for your success as a Business Growth Accountant?

The conscious use of cues (triggers, prompts, signals), or what Futrli refers to as 'alerts', helps you establish new success habits.

Your and your firm's ability to set up, nurture and grow habitual behaviours that support the work you do as a Business Growth Accountant are key.

As Hannah suggests:

> *"I would much rather, (accountants) pick up the phone and say, I know we haven't spoken to you in six months but we've noticed this thing has happened, are you okay? Wow, what an opener that is."*

The Power of Habit[53] by Charles Duhigg brilliantly summarises the research on the science of habit – especially the importance of cues (alerts).

You'll find more on habits in chapter 12 and in the 4-page Business Bitesize report on the resources page here – www.paulshrimpling.com/bga-resources Use this access code – **bga-resources2018** – to open the resources from this webpage. The shortened url is http://bit.ly/2plWsea

Small or large firms?

Evidence exists showing that larger firms[54] are doing better than smaller firms at business advisory work. However...

---

[53] *The Power of Habit by Charles Duhigg brilliantly captures the science of forming new habits. More on habits in chapter 12 and in the 4-page Business Bitesize report on the resources page here – www.paulshrimpling.com/bga-resources Use this access code – **bga-resources2018** – to open the resources from this webpage. Or visit http://bit.ly/2plWsea*

[54] *Statistics showing how £5m+ firms are better at billing advisory work than smaller firms show up in the report – The Good, The Bad, And The Ugly Of The Australian Accounting Profession. Go*

...the firms interviewed for this book are mostly small firms.

In short, both small and large firms succeed at advisory, so why not your firm?

It pays to think that the ability to adopt new approaches to client work, new cloud technology or indeed anything new can happen more quickly in smaller rather than in larger firms – just as a small boat turns faster than a tanker.

And yet a large £20m+ firm, Armstrong Watson, brilliantly transitioned 4,500 business clients onto Xero in just 12 months. That's almost 100 clients moved to Xero (on average) every week, an amazing and hopefully inspirational achievement.

So, large or small, the size of your firm is irrelevant.

As my friend Steve Pipe puts it:

> *"It's not the size of your firm that matters, but the size of your thinking"*

What actually matters most is whether you're serious about succeeding at being a Business Growth Accountant.

Half-hearted won't ever work for you.

---

here - http://www.gbuhq.com/click on the download tab in the menu and get yourself the executive summary for free.

Wholehearted will deliver you a Business Growth Accountancy business.

The individuals interviewed for this book were never short of passion, energy and commitment to their journeys toward becoming better and better Business Growth Accountants.

Small or large matters not.

My suggestion is just crack on, get stuck in and have a go at doing more advisory work. Set alerts up in your cloud accounting and cloud applications. Use these alerts to prompt you and your people to ask more questions, better questions, more valuable questions.

Ready to crack on?

Then it's time to get your pricing right...

11

How to price profitably

Before we get into the details of profitably pricing business growth accountancy work, meet Nigel.

Nigel Harris[55] accosted me at a recent event.

He insisted on telling me his pricing success story and even agreed to allow me to record his comments.

In short...

...he'd won 10 new clients in the last few months, at approximately £80,000 in fees. *If* he'd used his historical pricing process he'd have won some, but not all, of these clients, and at best the fees would have been worth £40,000, maybe £50,000. Nigel's words, not mine.

---

[55] *Nigel Harris is the owner of Harris & Co, London*

What Nigel had done was to give these prospects some pricing options, which helped make it easy for the client to choose.

If only pricing conversations were always so easy to manage.

The thing is, pricing conversations can be this easy to manage.

You just have to get your pricing process working well.

Avoid talking price?

Pricing conversations are usually avoided by most accountants.

Sending a price by email is much easier, much less stressful, much less confrontational, but much less successful.

Pricing conversations are generally avoided because of the fear, discomfort and lack of confidence in the pricing process.

If it was easy to talk about price, you'd have more pricing conversations, and better pricing conversations. And, based on my 16 years' experience, better pricing conversations will give you and your firm four big wins:

1. **Client loyalty will improve** because you'll be managing client expectations.

   Using email for communicating price does not manage the client's reaction to your price. Email a price and you're avoiding the one thing business owners (and all buyers) want to do – play the negotiation game. Giving clients the opportunity to quiz you on price nurtures discussion and develops confidence in you, your firm and the price.

Have a pricing conversation and you'll build better, stronger, more loyal clients. You'll be building capital value as a result.

2. **Cross sales will increase** because talking price is an opportunity to discuss options, extras and upgrades.

3. **You'll end up charging more** when you talk price because your client's confidence that they're getting a good price improves.

4. **You'll get more recommendations** by talking price because confident clients who are certain they have agreed a good price will feel less hesitation in recommending you.

Step up and talk price

You're responsible for pricing, not your business-owner client.

Even though accountants and business owners alike feel some degree of discomfort talking price, it's a valuable (emotionally-packed) conversation.

The issue is not the price.

The issue is your pricing process.

Build a better pricing process and you'll have better pricing conversations and get the four big wins listed above.

Even if you're getting comfortable with pricing, it's a safe bet that your fellow directors or managers need some help making pricing easier, better and more profitable.

Blind, deaf and dumb pricing?

I know I'm repeating myself in this section – but this issue is preventing your firm earning the fees and profits it deserves.

Pricing typically goes wrong, or delivers lower prices than it should, because you wear a blindfold, ear defenders and a gag when sharing your price with clients.

Most accountants prefer to share price by email rather than face-to-face.

This means you can't see or hear your client's reaction to the price. You can't help your client understand your offer, you can't answer any questions they have and you can't manage any unexpected issues.

Do whatever it takes to share price face-to-face and you remove the blindfold, ear defenders and the gag.

The key?

Start building your pricing conversation skills with prospective new clients.

Build a great pricing process for prospects. Build the *skill* in using the process with prospects.

You can then get the big wins of a better pricing process with all your clients, using the confidence you get from talking price with prospects.

Pricing Business Growth work with business owners needs more time and effort than pricing accountancy work because more trust is required for a business owner to say yes.

And if you remember the trust equation from the 'Right at the heart of it' chapter 4 you'll remember that increasing 'intimacy' is one the strongest ways to grow trust. More meetings foster greater 'intimacy' and gets you the four big wins of improved client loyalty, increased cross sales, higher prices and more referrals.

Surely not a one-night stand

Get your prospective new client to agree to two meetings:

1. A fact-finding meeting

2. A follow-up proposal meeting

How on earth can you establish a trusting relationship with a business owner in just one meeting?

No one agrees to get married after one meeting!

So why would a business owner commit to a valuable long-term Business Growth Accountant off the back of just one face-to-face discussion?

You might secure compliance work off the back of a single meeting, although the higher the fee, the less successful a one-meeting strategy will be for accountancy work.

Trusted relationships take time and require investment and commitment. A two-meeting approach sets you apart from most other firms and also builds a stronger (more intimate) relationship with the business owner.

Here's Steve Major, a chartered accountant in Australia, on delivering value in meeting 1 and setting up for a successful meeting 2 pricing conversation:

> *"...we've got to be looking at what outcomes the customer is wanting. So, before we go to actually determining the price...*
>
> *...we must have had those in-depth conversations where we've asked those detailed questions to understand what is really going on in their lives, in their business and that's going to give us the insight as to what outcomes, what deliverables they are wanting. Then, only then, can we start to look at actually setting the price."*

Also, it's worth using a concept I borrowed from the book 'Million Dollar Consulting'[56].

> *Your written proposal simply confirms what your client is expecting from you*

It's hard to profitably price in meeting 1 and it's not necessarily what you want. You want to get to meeting 2 in order to build a stronger relationship before having a valuable pricing conversation.

And it's worth remembering Ron Baker's sage advice when you're having your value and pricing conversations:

> *"Pricing is not a negotiation, and I believe firms should talk value and transformations first, price last."*

Then, in your email follow-up to meeting 2, you are simply confirming the level and the price agreed with your client from the meeting.

Multiple meetings, I realise, mean more effort, energy and more work. On the face of it, it looks harder.

But do you really want it to be easy?

---

[56] *Million Dollar Consulting by Alan Weiss is a great learning reference and worth adding to your library of resources.*

No, you don't want it to be easy

If it was easy to build a profitable pricing process, everyone would be doing it well and there'd be no competitive advantage.

But everyone isn't doing it.

Therefore, there's a competitive advantage waiting for you when you build a simple options document for clients, one you and your team can talk through.

Yes, it's easier for you to email prices, but does an email-pricing approach build trust and confidence in you as a Business Growth Accountant worthy of your client's trust?

Not really.

I appreciate that everyone is, to some degree, less than comfortable about talking price, especially if the price is higher than you're accustomed to or comfortable with.

But if you're serious about profitably pricing non-accountancy services, that is Business Growth services, then you'll need to manage, influence and help clients see the value in what you're doing for them.

You'll find it very hard doing this in an email.

You need to be face-to-face.

And just as more meetings make your pricing process more profitable, so does avoiding Hobson's choice.

Hobson's choice doesn't work well

In the 17th century, Thomas Hobson rented horses to Cambridge University students.

The students were offered just one horse – take it or leave it. And so was coined the phrase, 'Hobson's Choice'.

Who likes being given no real choice? Nobody.

When we're given Hobson's Choice, we mostly find a way to slow a decision down or avoid it completely. Your clients and prospects are the same.

We all resist 'Hobson's Choice' because of the deep-rooted, psychological need we all have to feel a sense of control. 'Hobson's Choice' removes our sense of control.

Knowing this, why would you want to offer a buyer just one price?

Providing your buyers with well-thought-out pricing options gives them a sense of control.

Pricing options also puts you in successful company:

- TripAdvisor

- Apple

- EasyJet

- Starbucks

Even if you already use tiered pricing options, as these companies do, there's more to price options than meets the eye.

Mastering the art and science of pricing options can seriously boost your business profits.

Profitable pricing options

Historically, it's been hard to get accountants to successfully offer three-option pricing for their accountancy work (accounts, personal tax, bookkeeping, payroll, etc.) in a successful and profitable way.

So, when it comes to pricing 'Business Growth Accountancy' work, we should probably expect more difficulty, challenge and frustration.

But pricing Business Growth Accountancy gets easier and works better when you use options.

Ever wondered why sale prices work so well? It's not because they are cheap, but because they are cheaper compared to the full price.

Offer only one price to a buyer and you make it difficult for them to assess the value, as they can't compare prices.

The thing is, they will compare prices anyway. They'll compare your offer with a competitor's offer, or compare your offer with a previous purchase. Offer just one price and you run the risk of losing out to your competition.

Provide options and you give buyers a reference point.

This relative reference makes it easier for them to make a decision in your favour – and you also put them in control. You win twice!

Here's Steve Major, again, who specialises in training accountants on pricing business advisory services:

> *"...too often, we just make it a yes, no conversation... We have a set of business advisory services that we present to a particular business and we put it all down and discuss a price, and that becomes a yes/no (decision).*
>
> *Whereas the far more powerful aspect of pricing is to understand how we buy. And one of the important aspects of how we buy, whether we're buying services or anything else, really, is we are making a comparison.*

263

> *...the person who's looking at purchasing business advisory services is going to... make some form of comparison, whether it's between accounting firms, whether it's between spending the money on business advisory services or spending this money somewhere else in his or her business.*
>
> *But they're going to make that comparison, so the easiest way to overcome that or to go a long way towards overcoming it, is to present the business owner three options, and three's the magic number."*

If you fail to provide options, your client will naturally seek other ways of comparing your 'Hobson's choice' price with other alternatives (from your competition?!).

Taking the pain out of pricing

Mark Upex, of Hansons Chartered Accountants in Yorkshire, raved to me in one meeting about how giving clients three options to choose from took all the pain and discomfort out of the pricing discussion.

Three options helped Mark feel less uncomfortable and helped his General Practice Doctor clients feel less uncomfortable too.

Creating three pricing options means you have to offer three levels of service. Therefore, you need to know the variables around which you're going to build your three levels or options.

Using the Higher-Value Route Map[57], shared earlier in this book, gives you a blend of variables you can use to create three options for your client:

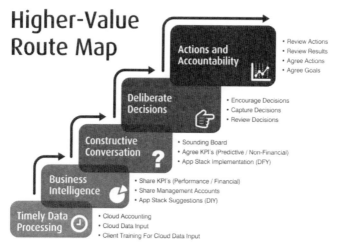

One of the main reasons that pricing advisory work can be tough is that you're pricing a series of meetings. You're charging to have a 'chat' with a client!

---

[57] A full-colour version of the 'Higher-Value Route Map' is available to you in the books free resources – use this access code – **bga-resources2018** – to get the resources from this webpage www.paulshrimpling.com/bga-resources

Charging for a conversation can feel, to begin with, a tad challenging.

There's something tangible about annual accounts and management accounts and payroll.

A friendly (but valuable) conversation feels harder to charge for. Especially when, historically, meetings and calls were something you throw in with the accounts and tax!

The Higher-Value Route Map above provides a simple, more tangible way of building three pricing options for your clients. The pricing variables show up in the bullet points of each step. I'm sure you can add to these bullets to create a process for getting to three price options.

IMPORTANT: Your price options will include the traditional accounting services and therefore give further substance to your three price options. However, it's more than possible that you can win advisory clients and charge £7,000 to £35,000 per year **with or without** accountancy wrapped in, as Andrew Botham at Mayes and Rob Walsh at Clear Vision Accountancy have done for more than a decade. Luke Smith, Greg Smargiassi, James Solomons and Steph Hinds are doing the same.

Keep it simple

Of all the firm's I've worked with on pricing, three things shine through for those firms who succeed at pricing well (profitably):

1. As the firms develop their three-tier pricing process, they learn to be brave when building their

options – they learn to charge more and more for meetings and calls.

2. If your pricing process is too complex and time-consuming, it will fail. It will fail for two reasons:

    a. If your pricing process is too complex, you and your people will not use it

    b. Your clients will be turned off and less likely to want to work with you

    Creating a single-page document with three price options and summary bullet-points for each option works best.

3. Success comes from using the single-page (on-screen or on-paper) three-tier options as a discussion document.

    Yes, it can be emailed after your meeting to confirm things, but the primary purpose of your single-page document of three options is to give you an agenda for a pricing discussion.

There are many important nuances around pricing that can either help or hinder your pricing process. Many books and courses are available to help you learn more.

One of the best pricing books is sign-posted in this 4-page Business Bitesize report – you can find a free copy at www.paulshrimpling.com/bga-resources Use this access code – **bga-resources2018** – to open the resources from this webpage. The shortened url is http://bit.ly/2plWsea

Learning more and more about pricing you should take deadly seriously, here's why...

Double your money

Going after knowledge on pricing and becoming an expert on pricing fits perfectly into a Business Growth Accountant's remit.

Why?

Because small changes to pricing can deliver significant profit improvements.

And pricing knowledge has two big payoffs:

1. You and your firm benefit from applying best-practice pricing

2. You're able to knowledgeably guide clients on improving their pricing processes too

For example, I know this is simple and basic, but it works. Ask yourself this question:

> *"How many clients would you lose if you added 1% to this year's planned price increase?"*

Just 1% more. Chances are you'd say you'd lose none (or very few) and yet you'd add 1% of turnover to your net profit.

Why not then ask the same question of a few clients and see what happens to the conversation?

Can +1% really deliver an 11% profit increase?

Two studies by McKinsey & Co and A.T. Kearny (both global consulting firms) suggest that *increasing your pricing has a bigger influence over your profits* than either reducing costs or increasing sales volumes.

	McKinsey	Kearny
Reduce fixed costs by 1%	+2.7% profit	+1.5% profit
Increase volume by 1%	+3.7% profit	+2.5% profit
Reduce variable costs by 1%	+7.3% profit	+4.6% profit
Increase price by 1%	+11% profit	+7.1% profit

Think - what impact could better pricing have on your bottom line profits and on the profits of your clients?

Advance your pricing knowledge

Each time you advance your knowledge on pricing, apply it to your firm and talk to clients about your new-found knowledge, you'll be helping yourself and your clients change one number.

If this number (the price charged) increases by 1%, it's possible you could be helping everyone achieve a 7% to 11% profit improvement.

It pays to know more and more about pricing.

Want more? Then dive into three brilliant books on pricing:

- 'Smarter Pricing – How To Capture More Value In Your Market' by Tony Cram

- 'Priceless – The Hidden Psychology Of Value' by William Poundstone

- 'Implementing Value Pricing: A Radical Business Model for Professional Firms' by Ron Baker

And check out anything online by Ron Baker[58] on value pricing – Google will get you there.

---

[58]*Ron Baker, in tandem with Intuit, created a very useful guide to pricing for accounting firms. You can use this link, but it is also easy to find using Google visit* http://intuit.me/2FNnJBq *but for the full url please see* – *http://http-download.intuit.com/http.intuit/CMO/accountants/accounting/2015/quickbooks/documents/quickopedia/intuit_webinars_resources_317.pdf*

Creating a process that shares three options helps you and your client talk around the options and allows you to help your client choose. The gift of choice might just get you increased (and quicker) referrals and cross sales and can help you win more clients at higher prices.

Make it easy for clients. The emotional impact of pricing discussions is often ignored or brushed under the carpet – even when pricing the traditional accounting services. Because emotions typically run high around pricing it pays to share prices in a meeting with your prospect or client.

If you're only sending pricing by email you are adopting the deaf, dumb and blind approach to pricing!

Sending a price by email is a cop out unless it simply confirms the price you agreed in your meeting.

And so, we come to meetings. Meeting management. Meeting habits.

Your meeting habits must support the work you do as Business Growth Accountant...

12

Your success autopilot

We finish with a chapter on building new habits.

Why?

Unless and until you turn your new Business Growth Accountancy behaviours into habitual behaviours, you'll be head-butting against your old habits.

With the right mindset, as described in chapter 5, you get the desire, commitment and zeal to make the changes you want to see.

But a growth mindset is not enough.

Goals aren't enough.

Desire isn't enough.

Here's why…

You're hooked on your old habits.

In fact, you're hard-wired to run your old well-established habits.

Even though you know you should change, you want to change, and you have a mindset for change, you're hard-wired to continue doing what you've always done.

How would you answer this question?

"If you always do what you've always done, won't you always get what you've always got?"

The answer is, of course – No.

In a fast-changing cloud-accounting world, continue to do what you've always done, and you'll end up with less. And you'll end up with less rather faster than you think.

Like Kodak. Kodak continued producing camera film whilst the rest of the world went digital – and Kodak went bust, despite having a cash cow with a near monopoly (and the patent for the digital camera!).

Here's your habit challenge

It's both a personal challenge and a challenge for your accountancy firm.

From the moment you wake up...

...you're on autopilot. As you stop the alarm on your phone, as you check your emails or social media...

...you're still on autopilot as you roll out of bed, stumble to the bathroom and run exactly the same bathroom routine you run every day, without thinking.

Your work-day breakfast routine?

The same routine every day, without thinking.

Your journey to work?

The same routine every day, without thinking.

Your greet-your-fellow-workers routine?

The same routine every day without thinking.

You could think of yourself as a *'human being'* or you could think of yourself as a *'HABIT BEING'!*

What we do, what we say and even what we think is dominated by the routines and habits we have established for ourselves.

Here's the rub.

Ultimately, your work habits determine your work success.

Your exercise habits determine your fitness success.

And your Business Growth Accountant habits will determine your success as a Business Growth Accountant.

Yes, autopilot is a good thing

...but only as long as your autopilot takes you where you want to go!

On a typical long-haul flight, a Boeing Dreamliner is on autopilot more than 95% of the time. The pilot has programmed the autopilot to get to New York from Sydney.

The human race is like the Dreamliner!

And like a long-haul plane we're mostly on autopilot.

But you have a choice!

Programme your autopilot (with your new habits) to take you where you want go or...

...allow your existing autopilot (your old habits) to do what you've always done (and get less and less as a result).

This is important because research suggests that between 95% and 50% of our daily actions are habitual[59].

I'd suggest the percentage is at the high end of the scale because it's not just actions (behaviours) that are habitual.

As well as behaviour habits, we have language habits and thinking habits.

---

[59] *Check out Charles Duhigg's book 'The Power of Habit' to get some deep insights into the science of habit and you'll start to see us as 'habit beings' too.*

For example, here's a language habit.

Please add the two words that finish the following sentence:

"Old habits ...."

Chances are, you either thought or said to yourself "old habits die hard". But – like John McClane (played by Bruce Willis) in the Die Hard film series – habits do not 'Die Hard'.

The science shows that habits NEVER DIE, just like John McClane never dies in four Die Hard movies!

~~*"Old habits die hard."*~~

"Old habits never die."

It's crucial you appreciate this because, even though new habits are essential for progress, it suggests that installing new habits is hard work. Really hard work. The odds are stacked against you.

You already know this based on the level of success you've not achieved with your New Year resolutions! Statistics show that 66% of new year resolutions fail[60] by 31st January!

---

[60]*https://www.theguardian.com/news/datablog/2015/dec/31/how-long-do-people-keep-their-new-year-resolutions* **The** *shortened url for this is http://bit.ly/2DEb2D4*

The neuroscience of habit

We touched on this neuroscience in an earlier chapter and it warrants repeating.

You can ride a bike, right?

If you ever learned to ride a bike, you'll always be able to ride a bike.

You know the well-known phrases (language habits):

"Once learned never forgotten...?"

"It's just like riding a bike...!"

The neuroscience of these phrases is connected to the production of myelin. Myelin forms around the brain fibres you use when you learn and eventually master riding a bike (or learn to draw, or learn to drive a car, or learn a new language or a new song lyric or advertising slogan, or learn any skill, for that matter).

Every cycle ride from your first to your last prompts your brain to wrap myelin round the brain fibres you use when riding your bike. By the time you have 50 myelin wraps[61] around your cycling brain fibres (50 cycling starts and

---

[61] *Research shows that a myelin-free brain fibre carries a brain signal at 2 miles per second. A brain fibre with 50 myelin wraps carries a brain signal at 200 miles per second! Check out the book 'The Talent Code' for a brilliant insight into achieving excellence in any skill, any sport, any activity.*

stops) you have hard-wired your brain to ride a bike to a very high standard.

It's the repeating behaviours that build myelin. Myelin hard-wires your brain and builds your new habits. Repetition is your best friend.

And as mentioned in chapter 5, making mistakes is a good thing if and when it prompts corrective action.

With 50 bike rides under your belt, even if you leave it for many years until you ride a bike again, you'll be able to pick it up really quickly. Yes, you'll feel a little 'rusty' when you first get back on a bike, but you'll soon be riding easily again. The myelin wraps may have faded a little – but only a little. A quick refresh and you'll be riding no-hands yet again!

So, to be successful at being a Business Growth Accountant you must install (whilst you're awake, conscious, deliberate and mindful) the habits of a successful Business Growth Accountant.

You must repeat (up to 50 times) the behaviours of a Business Growth Accountant and then you'll have laid down the myelin wraps and hard-wired the skill and become an expert Business Growth Accountant.

But you have a big battle to win!

Your 'old accountant's habits' are hard-wired already – many myelin wraps exist and they aren't going away.

The way you think, what you say and what you do to produce annual accounts for your clients are hard-wired as well.

You've run your 'old accountant's habits' many more than 50 times, which is why you find it so easy and natural to resort back to doing what you've always done.

The same goes for your colleagues too.

You're all battling your old habits.

The kids show the way

What's interesting is that children who know how the neuroscience of myelin works have been proven to learn better and faster than children who don't know this neuroscience of learning habits[62].

There's every reason to think this knowledge can help you and your firm too.

When establishing and nurturing new habits (with 2 miles per second brain signals) you are always battling against

---

[62] *From 'The Talent Code' by Daniel Coyle, quoting research by Carol Dweck the mindset expert. 350 of 700 children on an 8-week learning programme were taught the science of myelin and brain signal speed, they were shown that repetition pays off, and also that mistakes are part of learning and laying down more myelin. The teachers did not know which children were in the know and which were not, except that within a couple of weeks the learning behaviours of the 350 in the know became very obvious as did their improved results.*

your natural tendencies to resort back to doing what you've always done (with 200 miles per second brain signals).

It's a bit like an acorn trying to grow in the shadow of the big oak tree. It's tough. The acorn needs nurturing, bringing out of the shadow into the sun and rain and protecting from animals and bad weather!

So, you must nurture your new Business Growth Accountant habits. Thankfully, the science of habit suggests there's only a few habits on which to focus...

A few good habits determine your success?

Charles Duhigg in his powerhouse of a book, 'The Power Of Habit'[63], points to certain keystone habits.

Keystone habits are the few habits that have a profound impact on your success.

For example, on a personal level, Duhigg's research points to **parenting success** requiring the keystone habit of having meals together as a family.

---

[63] *Charles Duhigg's book 'The Power of Habit' brilliantly captures the science of forming new success-focused habits and is well worth a read. It will influence your skill and knowledge as a business growth accountant and help you help your clients be more successful.*

Health success is significantly connected to your keystone habit of exercise, because it also directly influences your eating habits!

This then prompts the question:

What keystone habits help you be a world-class Business Growth Accountant?

The right Business Growth Accountant Habits

Chapter 7 covers the keystone skill of asking great questions.

But what specific question habits can support you, help you and eventually make you automatically brilliant at Business Growth Accountancy?

It will pay you to revisit chapter 7 – Make Your Firm Truly Valuable – and look for ways to make asking great questions a habit.

Here are a handful of new habits to focus on:

- Work out your favourite opening business growth question and use it in every client meeting for the next three months (50 meetings!?). Use the start of every meeting as a time **trigger** for your new habit

- Use an alarmed diary appointment to **trigger** question preparation for each and every client meeting from now on

- Use the same alarmed diary appointment to **trigger** the preparation of a meeting agenda which then triggers great questions

- Habitually use the phrase '*tell me*' to **trigger** use of the six open questions when you're in conversation – What? When? Where? How? Who? Why?

The emphasis given to **trigger** in the four suggestions above points to the importance of establishing new success habits.

Cue, prompt, trigger, alert

Using triggers or cues or prompts to make you aware, awake and ready to use your new behaviour is one of the keys to establishing new habits.

Bolting new behaviours onto existing habits is a great strategy too – as long as you use the established habit as a **trigger** for your new habit.

For example, you may use an agenda already, so modifying your agenda by adding the agenda item 'growth goals and plans' will **trigger** questions and conversation about business growth.

For deeper insights into habits, I can't recommend Charles Duhigg's[64] book strongly enough.

But if you want an instant upgrade into the insights of habits, you can instantly access a 4-page easy-to-read Business Breakthrough report on habits here —

http://www.paulshrimpling.com/bga-resources and use this access code – **bga-resources2018** – to open the resources from this webpage. The shortened url is http://bit.ly/2plWsea

---

[64] *Charles Duhigg's book 'The Power of Habit' brilliantly captures the science of forming new success-focused habits and is well worth a read. Check out the report mentioned above to give yourself a quick start on this valuable topic.*

Cloud accounting meets the power of habit

Better than ever before, cloud accounting allows greater, easier and quicker access to relevant information about how well a business is doing.

And one vital element of cloud accounting helps you to be a Business Growth Accountant more than any other...

...because triggers are the key to nurturing and establishing new habits

...and triggers (from your cloud accounting apps) can start a brilliant business growth conversation.

Working as a Business Growth Accountant means you shouldn't be a cost to your clients. You should be delivering a significant return on investment (ROI). To deliver an ROI you must stimulate great conversations, great decisions and great actions that deliver great results.

Yes, questions enable a great conversation, but what stimulates or starts the conversation?

A trigger starts a conversation.

A trigger, a cue, a spark, a signal, a prompt.

The software world calls them **alerts**.

This is where the cloud accounting technology comes into its own – something that has been missing but is now one of your biggest helping hands.

For example, within Futrli software you can set up alerts for when cash drops below a set level. The email alert can then go to your client or to you or to the both of you.

You've then created an automated trigger to start a valuable (emotional) and timely conversation about something relevant and important.

You could even use these alerts to **trigger** some question preparation before you call or Skype or meet your client.

Here's suggestions from the Futrli team about the value of alerts (triggers):

> *"One of the key things that you would do as an advisor when you sit down with your client at the moment, to make you both responsible and accountable, is to set up some alerts.*
>
> *Really, we're looking at what thresholds, above and below within the business, are acceptable and what's not, and you can also have warnings around that."*

Can you see the value in this 'alerts' and 'threshold' conversation with your clients?

We mentioned this story earlier, describing the impact of using alerts on a business that initially refused to use their accountant as a business advisor:

> *"...one of the ways that one of our accounting partners in Australia has sold this technology to clients ...(is) he tried telling a client that he*

wanted to be his advisor, and it didn't really go down very well, even though he could see some really serious problems within this person's business.

So, what he did was go, "Hang on a minute. Well, I've done the research now. I've created a forecast. I've had a play around with (the numbers of) this client. What I'm going to do is set some alerts up."

When those alerts started pinging that the bank balance was falling into these critical areas that he wasn't happy with... he (started) picking up the phone and speaking to the client. Not only has he helped him turn around his business, but he's also grown his fees because that client was spending $1,000 a year with him and they now spend $12,000"

And, as already stated, better than ever before, cloud accounting allows more access, easier access and quicker access to relevant information about how well a business is doing.

Alerts within the cloud software can provide you with the new habit triggers you need to nurture, grow and strengthen your advisory habits.

Cloud software gives you an opportunity to deliver greater value (feelings) and earn the right to greater fees and profits too because of the timely access to relevant information, alerts and the client conversations these trigger.

Time to get started don't you think?

Time to ask a few questions, make a few mistakes and lay down some myelin on those Business Growth Accountancy brain fibres.

Time to apply your new learning (and learn some more).

I'd recommend you start asking a better question in your client and prospect meetings.

Revisit chapter 7 and work out which question you want to road test. And test it in your next meeting.

Remember...

"To know and not to do, is still not to know"

Zen saying

Here's a 30-day 'L-plate' how-to-get-started programme to help get you going...

Your 7-day / 30-day get started next steps...

This is a kick-start programme for you if you're new to doing work as a Business Growth Accountant.

You can also use the programme to work with a member of your team who is new to business advisory work.

Today Choose one friendly, open-minded client you can work with

7 days Book a meeting for the next week or fortnight

14 days Set two or three simple goals for your meeting

Prepare questions using the question frameworks in chapter 7

Prepare an agenda for your meeting and share it with your client

30 days Meet your friendly, open-minded client

Ask the questions you prepared. Listen purposefully and write down what you find out

Share your insights with your client, ready to discuss the next time you meet

Choose two more friendly open-minded clients you can work with and repeat the programme above or try the process with a prospective new client.

Also by Paul Shrimpling and the team at Remarkable Practice:

- **A weekly blog** – Check out Paul's weekly thoughts on the work he does every week with accountancy firms – you'll find the blog here – www.remarkablepractice.com/blog

- **Business Bitesize** – Paul also authors an easy-to-read bi-monthly business breakthrough report – you'll get free access to over 30 x 4-page reports by navigating our blog. Choose a blog that appeals to you and request the free Bitesize report that goes with it – www.remarkablepractice.com/blog. To get instant access to the Business Bitesize reports referenced in this book go to www.paulshrimpling.com/bga-resources Use this access code – **bga-resources2018** – to open the resources from this webpage. For the shortened url see http://bit.ly/2plWsea

- **The Business Growth Accountant Academy** is a skills training programme for owners of accountancy firms who want to grow and scale their firm's business growth fees and profits. The Academy includes workshops and video training for all owners, directors and managers of accountancy firms. And for ALL team members in your firm there's also a series of 2-5 minute bitesize skills videos providing a regular trigger to build skill, knowledge and insights for better client meetings and calls – find out more here – www.remarkablepractice.com/bga-academy

Books read and recommended by the contributors to this book:

The list of books below has been recommended by the experts I have interviewed for this book. I highly recommend you pick at least one of them and buy it right away from Amazon or your local bookshop.

You'll see that some of these book titles repeat from person to person. I thought you should see which titles repeat the most (Good To Great) so you can prioritise your learning...

Greg Smargiassi

- **What Got You Here Won't Get You There** by Marshall Goldsmith

- **Good To Great** by Jim Collins

- **Why Men Don't Listen & Women Can't Read Maps** by Allan and Barbara Pease.

Luke Smith

- **Winners** by Alistair Campbell

- **The Goal** by Eliyahu Goldratt

- **The 5 Most Important Questions You Will Ever Ask Your Organisation** by Peter Drucker et al

- **Influence – The New Science of Leading Change** by Joseph Grenny et al from Vital Smarts

- **Pricing On Purpose** by Ron Baker

- **E-Myth Revisited** by Michael Gerber

- **Turn Your Ship Around** by David Marquet

Rob Walsh

- **Good To Great** by Jim Collins

- **E-Myth Revisited** by Michael Gerber

- **Difference** by Bernadette Jiwa

Paul Shrimpling

- **The Trusted Advisor** by David Maister

- **The Power Of Habit** by Charles Duhigg

- **Good To Great** by Jim Collins

- **Humble Enquiry** by Edgar H. Schein

- **Mindset** by Dr Carol S. Dweck

- **Handling Difficult Difficult Conversations** by Douglas Stone et al

- **The Jelly Effect** by Andy Bounds

- **Influence – The Psychology Of Persuasion** by Robert Cialdini

- **Measure What Matters To Your Customer** by Ron Baker

- **The Talent Code** by Daniel Coyle

Steve Pipe

- **The Small Big** – Steve J Martin, Noah J Goldstein and Robert B Cialdini

- **Predictably Irrational** – Dan Ariely

- **The Heart of Success** – Rob Parsons

- **Accountants: The Natural Trusted Advisor** by Colin Dunn

- **What's Next For Accountants** – Shane Lukas

- **Effective Pricing For Accountants** – Mark Wickersham

- **True Professionalism** - David Maister

James Solomons

- **Start with WHY** by Simon Sinek

- **Good to Great** by Jim Collins

- **Who Moved My Cheese** by Dr Spencer Johnson

Paul Kennedy

- **The 7 Habits Of Highly Successful People** by Stephen Covey

- **Good to Great** by Jim Collins

- **Firm of the Future** by Ron Baker and Paul Dunn

Steve Major

- **True Professionalism** by David Maister

- **Good to Great** by Jim Collins

- **From Worst To First** by Gordon Bethune

One final thing...

I would really appreciate it if you would review my book on Amazon. Or if you prefer record your thoughts on the book purchase page of my home page for the book here - https://www.paulshrimpling.com/product/the-business-growth-accountant scroll to the bottom of this page to add your thoughts.

Also, you can drop me a line or ask me questions by emailing me at:

paul@remarkablepractice.com

index

A

ACCA, 27
Accountex, 27
AI, 44, 45
Alan Cowperthwaite, 8, 55, 75
Alan Weiss, 259
Alex Davis, 29, 232, 234
Alistair Campbell, 293
Allan and Barbara Pease, 293
Amanda Fisher, 29
Andrew Botham, 28, 72, 84, 92,
   141, 198, 211, 218, 223, 228,
   229, 266
Andrew Price, 235
Andy Bounds, 165, 294
Apple, 45, 262
Aptus, 32, 154
Armstrong Watson, 46
Artificial Intelligence, 44
AVN, 27
Aynsley Damery, 6, 28, 60, 89,
   127, 137, 142, 160, 197, 198,
   224, 228, 235

B

B1G1, 20, 29, 54
Bernadette Jiwa, 90, 169, 293
Business Bitesize, 27, 134, 148,
   203, 240, 250, 267, 291

Business Breakthrough, 27

C

canary analogy, 212
Carl Reader, 8
Carol Dweck, 119, 120, 123,
   124, 125, 126, 130, 200, 280
Carol S. Dweck, 119, 121, 294
Cedar & Co, 15
Chaplin, Simon, 42
Charles Duhigg, 250, 276, 281,
   284, 294
Clear Vision, 33, 85, 89, 93, 94,
   266
cloud accounting, 45
Colin Dunn, 295

D

Dan Ariely, 294
Daniel Coyle, 133, 134, 280,
   294
David Maister, 95, 96, 231, 294,
   295
David Marquet, 293
Davis Grant, 14
Douglas Stone, 294
Driver, Neil, 14
Dyke Yaxley, 15

Notes:

Notes:

Notes:

Notes: